Contents

Chapter 1 – Get motivated!   1

Introduction   2
1. Get real – where are you right now?   4
2. Get sorted   10
3. Get results   14

Chapter 2 – Know your own mind   21

Introduction   22
Stress   24
Balancing social life and study   29
Specific mental and physical conditions   31

Chapter 3 – Look after yourself   33

Introduction   34
Exercise   34
Sleep   36
Feed your brain   42
The effects of alcohol on learning   46

Chapter 4 – Tackling pressure head on   47

Introduction   48
What happens to our body when we're nervous?   50
Long-term coping strategies   52
Short-term coping strategies   57

Chapter 5 – Plan for success   59

Introduction   60
Setting up your space   60
Creating schedules and tracking progress   66

Chapter 6 – Take responsibility for your own learning   75

Introduction   76
Mindset   77
The importance of independent study   79
Study skills   80

Chapter 7 – Practise, practise, practise   97

Introduction   98
How to practise   100
LRP × 3   103

Chapter 8 – Get ready for the exams   111

Introduction   112
The last lap   113
A practical countdown to the exams   117
Summary   119

End notes   122

Chapter 1

Get motivated!

Lee Jackson

Lee Jackson has written books such as *How to Enjoy and Succeed at School and College* and is one of the most experienced and popular motivational school speakers in the UK. He has worked in schools for over 20 years and speaks in every type of UK school and college. His website is www.LeeJackson.biz.

Introduction

Help! I'm a motivational speaker! No seriously, I have one of the worst job titles in the world. People often don't know what to say to me at parties: 'Oh, right … erm … go on then, motivate me!' is a common response. But please don't be put off – I'm pretty normal really and I'm all about helping people like you to find the good stuff that can help them thrive in school. I'm not about strange theories and odd ideas, but the practical stuff and inspiring stories that could make a real difference to your exams right now.

What I'll tell you in this chapter is based on my experience and my work in schools. I'll help you get the right stuff into your head and your heart, so you can do the work to get the results that you *really* can achieve.

My reason for doing all the work I do in schools is simple. School is not an easy place to be sometimes, and most people don't enjoy exams. It's just something that we have to go through, to get somewhere else, like the job we want or the university course we're excited by. It's something that most of us *have* to do – so we may as well give it our best shot.

So, don't skip this chapter. I'll guarantee it'll help and it could make the difference between a pass and a fail.

The chapter is split into three main sections:

1   Get real

2   Get sorted

3   Get results

THEODORE ROOSEVELT
President of USA (1901–09)

'Do what you can, with what you have, where you are.'

1. Get real – where are you right now?

The first step in getting the best out of ourselves is pressing pause and asking the big question. Where am I right now?

If you've ever used maps on your smartphone or used a sat-nav, you'll know that it does three things.

   It finds out where you are.

   It asks you where you want to go.

and

   It prepares the best route for you.

But it can't do anything until it finds out where you are. Only when the phone has that information can it plan ahead and find the best route.

So, where are you? Be honest – I know it's not very easy, but it's so important …

Mark yourself (honestly!) from 1 to 10 on the scale opposite, where

1 = 'I don't put any effort in and I miss all of my teachers' targets'

and

10 = 'I'm hitting all my targets and I'm the perfect student'

Maths, English, Science:	👎 👍 1__2__3__4__5__6__7__8__9__10
The rest of my subjects:	👎 👍 1__2__3__4__5__6__7__8__9__10
Classroom behaviour/attitude:	👎 👍 1__2__3__4__5__6__7__8__9__10
My homework skills/effort:	👎 👍 1__2__3__4__5__6__7__8__9__10
I have fun at school:	👎 👍 1__2__3__4__5__6__7__8__9__10
My revision skills/effort:	👎 👍 1__2__3__4__5__6__7__8__9__10
How I get on with my friends in school:	👎 👍 1__2__3__4__5__6__7__8__9__10
How I get on with staff in school:	👎 👍 1__2__3__4__5__6__7__8__9__10

Get motivated!

Ok, great. When you've done that, then we know where you are and we can start to look forward.

What do you think about your exam chances right now? What grade do you think you'll get? Do you think you can get the results that the teachers have said you are capable of?

If you're confident then that's great – go for it. If you're not so sure, let me help.

Our beliefs are very powerful, they change the way we feel and the way we look and interact with the world around us.

Our mind works a bit like this:

THOUGHTS → BELIEFS → FEELINGS → ACTIONS

Our thoughts become our beliefs, our beliefs affect the way we feel and our feelings affect our actions.

Our beliefs change the way we see the world and how we interact with it. Bad beliefs can knock us out of shape. You might have seen the story of the turtle called Peanut (honest – it's real).

Peanut got the plastic holder from a six pack of beer caught over her shell and, because she wasn't able to remove it, she had it on for four years as she grew. Eventually she was found and freed from her plastic prison but this little piece of plastic litter had distorted her shell so much that she didn't grow and develop fully. A tiny thing changed her life. Bad and false beliefs are much the same – they seem tiny, but can affect us. Don't let thoughts or comments from people affect your future. Life is way too precious for that.

Our beliefs about ourselves affect our lives seriously. I've met people who believe that they are superior to others. This is not good – arrogance is a horrible trait that only leads to having no friends, being lonely and eventually a rude awakening. But the other side of the coin is no better, where we think very little of ourselves and feel like everyone is out to get us and we are worthless. This is even more scary and leads to all sorts of problems. Also not good.

But I think there is a middle ground, another way to get our beliefs right. To get them sorted.

It's called many things but I like to call it being **'realistically positive'**! It's doing what you've just done – finding out where you are, then believing the truth about yourself and then being positive for the future. If you're reading this book one day before your final exams it won't make that much difference, but if you're reading this weeks, months or even two years before your main exams it'll make a *big* difference. That's being realistically positive. We *can* do this school thing, but it'll take time, and time is a good thing – more on that a bit later.

So, what should we believe about ourselves? Well, as my friend and legendary youth worker Pip Wilson says – you are a beautiful human being (whether you feel like it or not!). Not a human **do**ing – we don't have to **do** amazing things to be worth something. Not a human **buy**ing – we don't have to **buy** expensive stuff in shops to be worth something. But a human **be**ing. We just have to 'be'. And the trick is to not let circumstances or others take that away from you.

That's because (and just in case you don't know!) you are a unique person, there's no one quite like you and there will be no one quite like you. Your life has purpose and meaning. And a big part of that purpose might just be at the other side of those exams. You might want to be the best engineer, the best midwife, the best games programmer or the best teacher. That will most likely involve more studying and getting the best results you are capable of. Otherwise your options may become limited or you'll have to re-take your exams later, which is never much fun.

Get motivated!

Let's just give our education a good go, otherwise it's just years of wasted time.

We can't travel back in time. But we can change our future. Starting now.

It's simple, but it won't be easy. Because simple isn't the same as easy. That's where hard work comes in. Something most of us don't like, but we know deep down makes sense.

A few small changes can add up to a better, brighter future.

Reflect:

The three things I'm going to take away from this section are:

1

2

3

WILL SMITH
Hollywood actor

'... if you stay ready,
you ain't gotta get ready,
and that is how I run my life.'

2. Get sorted

LeBron James is one of the best basketball players on the planet. He's a great scorer and a great defender. He can turn around a game in just a few minutes. He's won two championships. But what makes him stand out isn't his height or his dunking ability, it's the work he puts in. He has worked for many years to improve his skills in every area. Some players in the NBA are good at scoring but weak in other areas; LeBron has managed to be one of the best by understanding that he needs to put the hard work in to stay  that good. The main motto on his website is 'Just a kid from Akron, Ohio' but his other motto is 'Nothing is given. Everything is earned.' In other words, if he can do it anyone can do it. He is someone who has understood how to get the best out of his time as a player. He also did something amazing – over a period of seven years he got better and better *every* year! What if we could do the same?

Like LeBron, we have to commit to the journey we are on and make the changes we need to make to get even further. I'm sure LeBron doesn't get up every morning with a smile on his face and leap out of bed dancing to the practice court. He'll have bad days just like us, but he knows this and he has proven that when-he-does-what-he-needs-to-do he gets results.

We can too.

Once we know what we need to do, we can use the greatest gift we'll ever have to make change happen. And what gift is that? Time!

Time

Time works, it's always there; it can't be stopped, but it can be used for good.

If we flick the switch.

Flick the switch from wasting time, ignoring time and just hoping it will help us somehow without putting in the effort or changing anything.

You can flick the switch now.

Flick it to 'I know where I'm at, so I now know what I need to do.' Once we know what to do to make a difference, we can use time well. It becomes our friend, not our enemy.

For example: you know that you need to do more revision for the next exam coming up. Decide that, get it done and see what happens. Did you get a better result straight away? Hopefully. But if not, keep on with the revision and watch your results get better and better as time passes. In sport they call it marginal gains. Going back to LeBron James – he couldn't become a better scorer overnight, but with the right effort he improved every week, bit by bit, basket by basket.

Remember, to really make it happen we have to take responsibility for our studies and commit to changing our sometimes not-so-good habits. Otherwise nothing will happen. Wishing something will change has never helped anyone, but doing something different and for the better has *always* delivered results. (See chapter 6 for lots more on how to take responsibility for your own learning.)

But before you panic, thinking all this work seems endless – remember that this doesn't last forever *and* you get time off too. You can enjoy as much time off as you want in the holidays and when you are off school with no exams coming. But the key to enjoying those holidays is to work when you know you need to – knowing in the back of your mind that a day off or school holidays are never far away.

Get your team sorted

I know we are talking about individual success at school here but we need a team to get us there. Everyone has a team, even if they don't know it! LeBron James has an army of coaches and trainers helping him. When I'm doing talks in schools I often talk about the BBC show *The Apprentice*. You know – the one where a load of wannabe business people who've just bought a new suit and think they can be Lord Sugar's next big thing make fools of themselves. It's an entertaining show at times but for me it's not about business, it's about entertainment. Because business just isn't like that. I have a couple of friends who've been on the show and they told me how it's filmed: it's non-stop, it's relentless and it's edited to make it seem more exciting than it is most of the time. Especially the funny things they say in the boardroom, which is filmed over several hours, not just ten minutes like we see! I hate the way they always seem to lie, cheat and have a go at each other. Because what the show forgets to say is that it takes a team to build a business. It takes a team to get you through school, too. So, who's in your team? Your parents or carers, your friends, your subject teachers, your head of year, your form teacher, your mentor, your youth worker, the librarian at school … the list goes on.

If you stop and think now I bet you can name your team. Why not write their names down on a blank piece of paper with your name in the middle? A bit like this, but bigger …

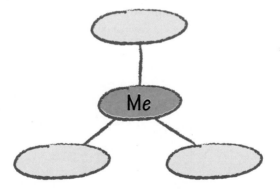

But remember, if you want to get even better results, you might need to get someone else on your team. You might need to shake your team up a bit; some people might need to be put on the subs bench too. Your team is people who help you to do well, not people who put you down or who don't see the value in you doing well at your studies. You don't want to be hanging out with a load of negative friends who aren't bothered about their studies as that won't help you.

Now, don't get me wrong – most of what we need to do is always in our heads, but a good team will help us get there more easily. Choose your team carefully. Use them to boost you towards exam success.

Reflect:

The three things I'm going to take away from this bit are:

3. Get results

Now you know where you are and you've got stuff more sorted, it's time to see yourself through to the results you deserve. But the end of your course may be months, if not years, away. So how do we #keepongoing until that time?

Here are a few tips:

Keep on moving.

The key is to keep on moving. Because when we are moving we are being active and our brain is more engaged. If we spend ages doing nothing for school, it slows our progress down and gets us into bad habits. Of course we all have times where we need to rest, but successful students learn to keep active, too. And I mean that literally – i.e. do some activity, go to the gym, take a walk, play netball or football. Keeping moving helps our bodies and our brains to stay healthy. I don't feel so good when I haven't exercised for a few days; it's part of life's natural rhythm, move and rest, revise and rest, revise and run even! All at the same time, if you're really skilled at juggling! In fact, even when you are revising, it's best to have a rest and change your scene – so do half an hour, then get a drink or run up and down your street. Anything to keep your brain active.

Put (the right stuff) **in** (to) **the hours.**

Don't just put in time, that's a given. Even more important is what you put into the hours you do work. It's so easy to get distracted on YouTube or by the radio or the TV when studying. We need to put the right effort into the hours we do have. Get your stuff ready, switch off your distractions, and then be tough enough with yourself to just keep on working *without* distractions. Working for your exams means doing it *uninterrupted*, and the easiest way to do this is by finding that special button on your phone, that magical button (you know the one!) that turns your phone off! If we are constantly interrupted, information just doesn't go into our brains properly. Switch your phone and your distractions off, get your work done and then switch them all back on again. Simple. Twenty minutes of concentration is far better than two hours of taking apart your colour pens and drawing the most complex doodle known to man! That's nice, but it won't help you pass exams. Sorry :)

WILL ROGERS
Hollywood actor

'Even if you're on the right track, you'll get run over if you just sit there.'

Get motivated!

Make things happen, don't just get things done.

It's easy to get stuff done. To tick little things off a list, easy stuff, but the key is to make things happen.

Do the big stuff **FIRST!**

If you've written a list it might look a bit like this:

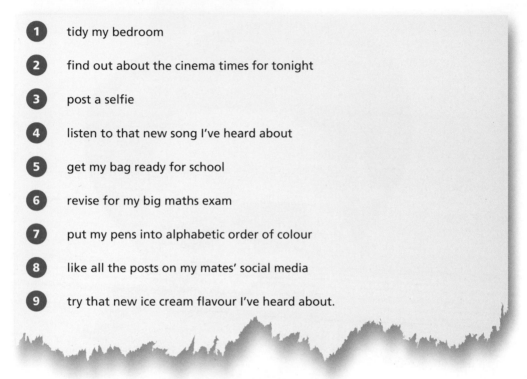

1. tidy my bedroom

2. find out about the cinema times for tonight

3. post a selfie

4. listen to that new song I've heard about

5. get my bag ready for school

6. revise for my big maths exam

7. put my pens into alphabetic order of colour

8. like all the posts on my mates' social media

9. try that new ice cream flavour I've heard about.

If we just want to get things done then we'll do 1, 2, 3, 4, 7, 8 and 9. We'll be busy and feel like we've done stuff. But really 5 is pretty important – and 6 is the biggie. Author Brian Tracy quoted Mark Twain and famously called it 'Eat that frog' – we have to learn to do the big stuff first and do the other stuff when we have finished or when we are on a break from the big stuff or even not at all.

Don't be busy just working hard. Work smart. Do the big ugly frog-shaped stuff first, and the other stuff will take care of itself. The key is to do what we *need* to do, because there is never enough time to do everything we *could* do.

Stay positive +

We all have good times and not-so-good times, we have good days and not-so-good days. That's called life. But what we can do is learn to be more positive than negative. The world bombards us with negativity and people do, too. But a key to life is to be tough enough on the outside to keep on going while still being soft enough in the middle to enjoy life, family and friends. You will have bad days at school between now and your final exams but after a bit of a sulk you need to find your way out of that, because a new day starts when you decide it does. We can draw a line and start afresh anytime we want. So find out what gets your head in a more positive place and use it. It might be some of the advice from this book, getting outside, playing sport, chatting to your mates, having a sleepover. Whatever it is, use these things to stay positive. I can guarantee you this – a positive state of mind will *always* get you a better result. That is a big truth, that I've learned the hard way. Positive and determined is a great way to be. Find ways to stay like that or to get yourself back to that good place. (You'll find great strategies for staying positive in chapter 4.)

A quick history lesson:

During the Second World War (1939–45) something was built that was a massive secret and hardly anyone knew about until afterwards. It was called the PLUTO pipeline. PLUTO stood for **P**ipe **L**ine **U**nder **T**he **O**cean.

This top secret war mission laid several pipelines under the sea from the Isle of Wight all the way to France where our troops were starting the big push to beat the Nazis in what was called D-Day and the Normandy landings. The fuel that these pipelines carried helped the Allies win the war. They kept the troops going, they were a sign of hope. These secret pipes made a massive difference to the invasion and eventual victory.

What is the positive pipeline that keeps you going? The people and things that keep you positive in challenging times like the run-up to exams may be invisible to some, but they are important just the same.

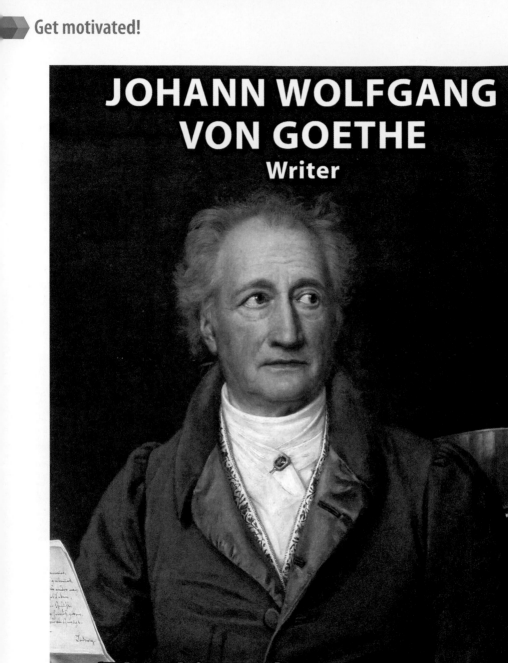

JOHANN WOLFGANG VON GOETHE
Writer

'The things that matter most must never be at the mercy of the things that matter least.'

Finish well!

Finishing well just means keeping on going until the job is done. It's about taking action, the action that you know deep down is right. Life is better when you take responsibility for your actions, and pursue your studies and life with a real purpose and passion. Nothing compares to 'the rush' of crossing the finish line.

Imagine, now, that time in August when you get the results you've worked hard for :)

Here's a **10 point plan** to make those results look even sweeter ... tell it to yourself, now and often.

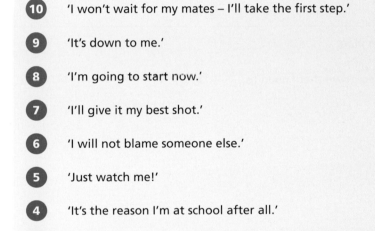

10 'I won't wait for my mates – I'll take the first step.'

9 'It's down to me.'

8 'I'm going to start now.'

7 'I'll give it my best shot.'

6 'I will not blame someone else.'

5 'Just watch me!'

4 'It's the reason I'm at school after all.'

3 'As Nike says, I'll Just Do It!'

2 '"I will", not "I might" but "I will"'.

1 'I know that it's **"Me"**. Not "them", but **"Me"** that'll make it happen (I **AM** going to do this).'[1]

Find *your* way to finish strong. The rest of this book will help.

#keepongoing

Get motivated!

Reflect:

The three things I'm going to take away from this last bit are:

1

2

3

Fill this in, it might help:

> **My quick, effective action plan:**
>
> Starting today I know deep down that I need to:
>
> **1**   Do more …
>
> **2**   Do less …
>
> **3**   Prioritise …
>
> **4**   Talk to …
>
> **5**   Get help with …
>
> I **will** do the above (because I know it'll help my studies and let me have more fun too).
>
> Signed:
>
> Dated:

Chapter 2

Know your own mind

Know your own mind

Nicola Morgan

Nicola Morgan is the author of nearly 100 books, including the award-winning Young Adult novels *Wasted*, *Fleshmarket* and *Mondays are Red*. A former teacher and specialist in dyslexia, in the last ten years Nicola has become widely known for her passionate work on adolescence, with her 2005 book, *Blame My Brain – The Amazing Teenage Brain Revealed*, being shortlisted for the Aventis prize and her recent title, *The Teenage Guide to Stress*, being snapped up by teenagers and their hard-pressed adults. Both titles have been translated into various languages and Nicola now writes and speaks internationally on a range of subjects relating to adolescence, learning, stress and the reading brain.

Introduction

The human brain is an amazing machine which sometimes doesn't work as brilliantly as we would like it to. There are times when we especially need it to work at its best – exams and tests are obvious examples – and many factors affect whether our brain has a good day or not. Some of those factors we can't control – being ill, for example, or sudden bad news – but there are many we can control, once we've learned how.

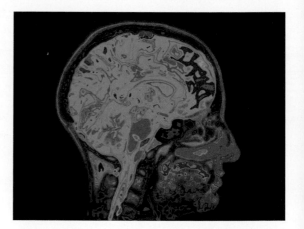

When athletes are preparing for a major competition, their coaches help them work on all aspects of their lives: nutrition, sleep, stress levels and mental state, as well as practising the actual sport. Coaches will be very scientific, using the most up-to-date research about how bodies perform best. As you prepare for exams, it's a good idea to have the same attitude, working on both your body and mind, so that they can produce peak performance on the day.

The best way to start this training is to understand what factors affect performance. Most of these are the same for everyone, because our brains all work in the same basic way, but we do have different strengths, weaknesses and habits and it's useful to start to notice what makes *you* more likely to remember and understand what you're learning, and more able to produce it in a test or exam.

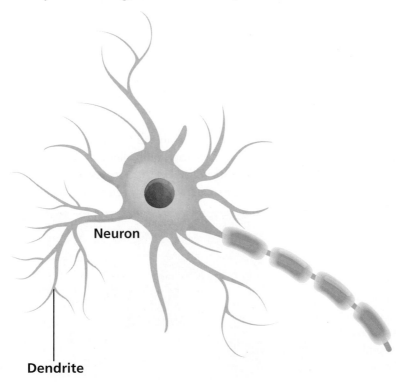

Neuron

Dendrite

Key Point

An important point about how the brain works:

Everything we do, from the simplest to the most complicated, requires the right brain cells ('neurons') to connect through a network of branches ('dendrites') so that electric signals can pass along the networks. The first time we try a new skill, the pathways are weak but, each time we try, the dendrites grow and the connections become stronger. As we practise more, the pathways become stronger, the signals can move more efficiently, and the task becomes easier. That's how learning happens and why practice is so important: each time you practise, the necessary connections grow physically stronger.

Why do different people find things easy or hard?

Lots of things affect how easy it is to learn something: mood, energy, concentration, confidence, the way you're taught, specific skills you already have. Someone who is under a lot of stress on a particular day, or feels ill, or had a bad sleep, or has had a confidence knock, may find it harder to absorb new information. Someone with strong networks in the brain areas used for maths will find it easier to learn a new maths concept; someone with strong networks in some language areas will find certain word-based tasks easier.

By the time you approach exams, you'll know your strengths and weaknesses, because many of your brain networks will have been established during your schoolwork over the last few years. What we need now is to get your brain (and the rest of your body) into a state in which it can work as well as possible during your revision months and then do you justice on the day.

Stress

Stress is not actually a bad thing: it's the body's natural response to a threat or challenge, producing chemicals (especially adrenaline and cortisol) to make blood rush to our heart, brain and muscles and make us focus acutely on what needs to be done. It is designed to produce peak performance.

You might have heard of the 'fight or flight' response. This is something all animals (including humans) need in order to escape danger or fight back to defend themselves. If our ancestors hadn't had this biological response they'd have been more likely to have been eaten by predators. They also wouldn't have been able to chase prey fast enough to catch it. So, we need stress for survival.

While this chemical reaction helps us achieve peak performance in the face of a challenge or danger, it also makes us feel uncomfortable. Everyone has experienced feeling nervous before a race, test, interview, public performance, even just speaking in front of the class: we feel tense and jittery; we might feel sick; we might describe 'butterflies' in our stomach or need the toilet; we may be snappy; we'll find it hard to sit still. These symptoms are a perfectly normal part of this chemical reaction. If we felt too comfortable, we probably wouldn't get up off the sofa!

When the reason for stress (the 'stressor') passes, adrenaline and cortisol levels drop and we feel better. That's what is supposed to happen anyway. Let's look at why a problem sometimes arises and we start to 'suffer from stress'.

When does stress become a problem?

 When it's constant, without relief, so the chemicals can't die down and cortisol builds up. This is the problem with modern life: many of us, including most teenagers at school, are bombarded by frequent small stressors. We are constantly alert, fretting, ready for action which doesn't always happen, so the stress doesn't have a natural release.

2 When it's too powerful, producing panic instead of action. When you panic, you can lose sight of the sensible action to take, miss obvious answers and make mistakes.

A useful way to visualise how stress can cause problems is to imagine there's a certain amount of stress your body can deal with in one day – let's say one glassful. When you wake in the morning, ideally that glass is empty because you have no stress. In fact, it probably won't be empty as you'll be carrying some stress from yesterday, or you had a bad sleep or upsetting dreams. So, already there's a bit of stress in the glass. Then, as each stressor happens – tiny things like not being able to find your shoe, moderately annoying things such as your brother spilling milk on your phone or your mum shouting at you to hurry up, and bigger things such as someone being foul to you on the bus or being late for a class or getting a bad mark or discovering that you haven't been picked for the school play – your glass of stress fills up. If you can't reduce those stress levels, it's going to overflow. Or it won't be empty next morning because one night's sleep may not be enough to remove the chemicals.

How stress and anxiety can affect learning

When you're stressed, imagine parts of your brain being occupied with worrying, which may well include the parts you also need to use for your work. So you'll find it harder to focus on your tasks. You might have heard of 'multi-tasking' but research shows[2] that if we're occupied with one task, we cannot perform another task as well as if we were focusing on it alone. (Some tasks become automatic and we can manage them at the same time: for example, expert drivers

can talk and drive, but if something happens that means they have to focus more on their driving, even they will stop talking.) So, thinking about something (a worry) will affect your concentration.

Emotions may play a part in learning, too, and some learning tasks may be easier when we are feeling good. Some research suggests that we think more creatively when we're happier.[3]

Know your own mind

One stress that young people often suffer is low self-esteem, feeling you're useless or that you'll never be able to understand or learn the work. Most people know that feeling. Trouble is, if you really convince yourself that you're useless, it will be even harder to succeed. When we believe we can do something, we often find we can. So, somehow you need to banish those 'I can't do it' thoughts, and replace them with 'I can if I break it into steps.' There's advice about this elsewhere in this book, in chapter 4 and chapter 6.

How to recognise when you're stressed and anxious

Some of these things will be obvious, but others might not be. If you suffer from the following, they are often a sign of stress:

- Regular headaches, stomach-aches and/or dizzy spells. (You should check with your GP first, but it's likely that it's stress-related.)
- Pain in shoulders, jaw or neck, often caused by not realising you're tensing up those muscles. (Again, check with a GP first.)
- Appetite problems – either having no appetite or binging on 'junk' food – and weight changes.
- Intrusive negative thoughts.
- Clumsiness – common in teenagers even when not stressed, but can also be because you're preoccupied with other things.
- Frequent colds and other minor illnesses – when cortisol builds up it can affect your immune system and make illnesses more likely.
- Feeling constantly overwhelmed by how much you have to do and feeling panicky about it.
- Being very snappy and saying things you don't mean.
- Sleep problems – either not being able to get to sleep or waking very early.
- Other things that are making you worried about your state of mind – see a GP, who can check you out, reassure you and give you strategies for recovery. Hearing voices, pulling out hair, strange thoughts – whatever it is, you're not alone, and there is help for you.

Anti-stress strategies

There are lots of ways to reduce stress. I have split them into three categories:

 Instant strategies
- Learn a breathing/relaxation exercise – there are good audios around, to download[4] or buy.
- Learn to visualise a calm, beautiful place – again, there are audios to guide your imagination.
- Use those strategies to deal with panic, to wind down before sleep and any time you want to feel more relaxed. Practise till you can do them automatically.

2 Daily relaxation
- Build at least half an hour into your day for something that relaxes you, such as: having a bath, going for a walk, having coffee with a good friend, meditating or practising mindfulness.
- Make sure you spend some time each day with both internet and phone switched off – you'll be amazed how relaxing it is!
- Have a hobby. You might think you're too busy for hobbies now that exams are approaching, but you're wrong. A hobby will give your brain time to let your work settle in and when you return to the work you'll be able to tackle it better. Brains like variety. There's a phrase, 'A change is as good as a rest' – it's true!
- Keep reading for pleasure – it's relaxing, takes your mind off your problems and helps you wind down before sleep. It's good for the same reason as a hobby is but there's also very good research[5] that suggests that daily reading for pleasure is linked to better exam results. (It might be that people who are good at exams read more, rather than reading making you do better in exams, but it's still interesting.)
- Exercise every day (but make sure you eat afterwards, to build up your energy). See pages 34–36.

- Whether a hobby, reading or sport, give yourself time each day in which you find 'flow'. This is the feeling of being completely engaged in a particular activity or task, so engrossed that you don't notice what's going on around you. It's sometimes called 'engagement' and is reckoned to be a very important part of wellbeing and mental health.[6]

3 Lifelong attitude
- Remember that whatever you're worried about, you're not alone. And you're not weird! Someone else has the same worry, I promise.
- Talk to someone – find a trusted adult. If it's your parent, great, but it doesn't have to be; sometimes you may not want to open your dark thoughts to them, or you might think you'll upset them too much. Teachers are trained in how to help you – or to help you find someone who can. And you can always see your GP: you can make an appointment yourself. Or talk to Childline, who guarantee 100% confidentiality; either phone free (0800 1111) or go online.[7] If you use the internet at home you may want to clear your browsing history – there's information on the Childline website about this.
- Understand that everything passes: things that seem enormous now just won't after a while. We all know the feeling of being overwhelmed by the moment, but this feeling does pass.
- Realise that relaxation is not a luxury: it's how to be healthy and make your brain and body do their best for you.

Balancing social life and study

Sometimes it can feel as though *everything* is about exams at the moment, with constant reminders about their importance from school, home, the media and friends. Teachers and parents don't mean to put you under too much pressure and may not realise they're doing it, or they may just feel it's their job to keep you focused. It can seem as though there's either no time for social life or that adults want you to put your social life on hold till exams are over.

Some of you might also be juggling a really difficult home situation and you may feel that social life is simply not a priority. You may not even feel like chatting to friends, especially if they aren't going through the same problem as you.

Meanwhile, friendship groups can be causing problems that are nothing to do with exams. Or perhaps you fear that if you don't spend time with your friends they will lose interest in you and you'll be cut out. These are all very understandable concerns.

The good news is: keeping your social life and connections going is important! As long as you want to, of course: some people prefer to be alone and that's fine as long as you have someone to talk to if you want to.

Spending some time with friends, ideally face-to-face, has several benefits:

- It allows you to share worries with people going through the same things, people who understand.
- Or it lets you switch off from your worries for a while and have fun. Just as I said when discussing hobbies, varying your mental activity is a very good idea and will help you revise and work better.
- There's interesting research that suggests that having a social, face-to-face conversation may be useful in allowing the brain to remember recent learning.[8]

- Even if you aren't actively worrying about things, the brain likes variety and you will return to work refreshed.
- Although many people value time on their own, there's a phrase (from a poem by John Donne) 'No man is an island': humans operate best with support groups. So, even if you don't want to spend lots of time with your friends, you will benefit from knowing that you can talk to them if necessary. A support group or a good friend doesn't have to be someone you see daily if you don't want to, but you should if you need to.
- It's not only about the support your friends can give *you*: giving support yourself will improve your own wellbeing. Psychologists know that we benefit from helping other people.[9]

But *how* can you do this when you're so busy?

It's hard but I believe it's important. Managing social life and interaction with friends is a key part of maximising your mental health during a very stressful time. And your brain will thank you. So, here are some tips:

- If your parents realise you are taking your work very seriously, they will accept that you need to hang out with friends sometimes. Work *then* play!
- Plan your social life within your revision timetable: one evening a week when you relax with friends? A weekly trip somewhere fun, such as the zoo or ice-skating? A daily chat with your best friend?
- Agree with your closest friends that you won't interrupt each other's revision but encourage each other by looking forward to coffee or a meal in one of your houses or a cinema trip once you've done your work that week.
- Among your friends, pair up as 'stress buddies' (it doesn't have to be pairs – it could be threes or fours) and agree to look out for each other. Commit to check daily to make sure everything's OK.
- But make sure everyone realises that if you are really concerned about a friend, you will talk to an adult. You are not responsible for your friends' health.
- When something goes wrong in your friendship group, try to put the whole thing in perspective: is it really worth falling out over? Who can be the one with the big heart and make a peace offering? It could easily blow over in a few days.
- A social life that involves abusing alcohol is the worst thing you can do to your brain and health. Do everything to avoid it. (See page 46 for the problems that alcohol causes for the brain.)

In short, it's about putting work first but also realising that you'll work better if you break it up with other things, including being as social as you want to be.

> **Key Point**
>
> The world of social media is wonderful. But a big problem is the time involved. How sick would you feel if you realised you'd spent a huge number of hours (they mount up!) on social media and your exams went badly? So, set strict limits and only go on social media when you've done an amount of work you feel good about.

Specific mental and physical conditions

Several factors personal to you might make your revision more challenging. Don't be daunted, as there are lots of ways you can get help. You will already know if you have any of these conditions and you should have a good understanding of them. Now it's just a matter of working out whether you need to make any adaptations for exams.

For *all* the conditions I'm about to list:

* Make sure teachers properly understand the situation. This should be the job of your Year Head, or whatever your school calls the person with overall responsibility for your learning.
* Ask for help *early*.

Dyslexia (and related conditions such as dyspraxia and dyscalculia)

* Make sure you have the necessary extra help in place long before exams. You need formal assessments before you can have extra time or special equipment, so make sure your Learning Support (or equivalent) teacher has this in hand.
* Organisation and planning may be tricky for you, so ask for help with this.
* Break all learning tasks into small sections. Better to learn some things well than struggle to tackle everything and fail.
* Look out for study guides especially aimed at people with dyslexia, etc.

OCD and other extreme anxieties

* Make sure your GP and/or counsellor has discussed with the school what help and support you need.
* Make sure you have enough of any medication you take.
* Trust my stress strategies on pages 27–28 and be prepared to utilise them frequently and confidently.

Depression

* Ask for special advice from your GP and any counsellor you are seeing.
* Set small targets and reward yourself often.
* Make yourself take a brisk walk every day.
* If you take medication, make sure you have enough, and do not stop taking it unless advised by your doctor.

Bereavement or any difficult family situation

- Be kind to yourself. Do not expect too much. If you are going through a really difficult time, everyone will understand if you don't perform as well as you deserve. There will be time to try again.
- Accept all help offered – people want to help. And if people don't offer, because they don't know what you need, ask. It can be really hard for people to say the right thing, so try to be as open as possible, then you'll get the support you need.

Brain injuries causing memory difficulties (for example)

You might know that you are weak in a particular skill, perhaps after a childhood illness or head injury. But the good news is that brains are very adaptable and, with lots of effort and time, you can rebuild these skills. Meanwhile, the following tips could help:

- Break down all tasks into very small steps and tackle them one at a time.
- Develop a system whereby you make a note of what you've learned or worked on, so you can see what you've done and note progress.
- Memory works best when we keep revisiting the material, with increasing gaps of time. So, when you first learn it, revise it the next day, then three days later, then a week later, then a month later. This is called 'spaced repetition'. You'll find much more about this in chapter 7.
- Set realistic targets, never impossible ones.
- Don't spend too long on one task – break up work with other activities, including exercise or a hobby. This is true for everyone, but particularly for you.

Asperger's Syndrome

Everyone with Asperger's is different so it's hard to generalise. You may well be highly organised and good at concentrating. Or, you may find it very hard to switch off your worries, and find yourself unable to focus on the right thing. Some of these tips might help – choose the ones that feel right for you:

- You probably have a good understanding of yourself by now, so try to work with your strengths but be aware of your problems.
- Don't be surprised if friends and classmates have less patience – they are wrapped up in their own stresses. It's not personal.
- People with Asperger's are as likely to suffer stress as anyone and will respond to the same strategies: again, pick the ones you like the sound of.

For all of you: keep remembering that once these exams are over, you'll be able to drop your least favourite subjects and focus on your strengths.

Also, to recap, although stress is there to make you perform well when you get to your exams, you will notice huge benefits if you manage to give that stress some breaks, so that the chemicals can reduce and give your body and brain a chance to prepare for exam day.

Look after yourself

Nicola Morgan

Nicola Morgan is the author of nearly 100 books, including the award-winning Young Adult novels *Wasted*, *Fleshmarket* and *Mondays are Red*. A former teacher and specialist in dyslexia, in the last ten years Nicola has become widely known for her passionate work on adolescence, with her 2005 book, *Blame My Brain – The Amazing Teenage Brain Revealed*, being shortlisted for the Aventis prize and her recent title, *The Teenage Guide to Stress*, being snapped up by teenagers and their hard-pressed adults. Both titles have been translated into various languages and Nicola now writes and speaks internationally on a range of subjects relating to adolescence, learning, stress and the reading brain.

Introduction

Your brain is in your hands! Although you can't control everything about it, there is a lot you can do on a daily basis to make it work as well as possible and help you get the best results you're capable of. Exercise, sleep and good nutrition all have a huge role to play in your health and success.

Exercise

The health benefits of exercise are strongly accepted in the medical and scientific community.[10] It's fairly obvious that exercise is good for your bodily strength and your heart, but it's also great for mental health. Exercise is prescribed for both depression and anxiety and we have plenty of evidence[11] – based on research and what people report – that it's a very good way of preventing the bad effects of stress and dealing with it when it happens.

What are the benefits of exercise?

- Physical activity increases oxygen to the brain.
- Vigorous exercise releases 'endorphins' in the brain – these are often called 'happy chemicals'. This can explain the feeling of euphoria you can get after going for a run or doing an intense workout.
- Psychologically, you feel good about yourself because you know you did something beneficial.
- It gives you a break and a change from 'brain work'.

- Some exercise (things you do on your own, such as running or gym workouts) gives you time to think things through.
- Other exercise (things you play in teams) gives you social opportunities.

Key Point

A word of warning: people with eating disorders such as anorexia nervosa often use exercise to burn calories. Over-exercising is harmful. It's bad for your joints, especially if they are not supported by enough muscle, and uses the energy you need to work. As I say in the section on food, restricting food and energy intake without medical supervision will not allow your brain to work well for you.

What exercise works?

It depends what suits you. But it doesn't have to be unpleasant!

- A brisk walk is brilliant exercise – it pushes more oxygen round your body, takes you away from your screen and your books, and gives you thinking time. I find when I have to learn something (such as a speech) or think through a new idea, walking is the solution.
- Yoga and Pilates are great for relaxing your mind as well as strengthening muscles – and, because your heart rate doesn't raise much, they are ideal before bedtime.
- Any exercise that's part of a hobby, such as team sports or something like tennis, is a great stress reliever and all-round health-promoter, helping take your mind off things.

- If you can build exercise into your daily or weekly routine, it will be easier to remember.
- The NHS recommends[12] an hour a day for young people aged 5–18, with a mixture of moderate exercise such as walking, more vigorous exercise such as sport, and muscle-strengthening activities.

After exercise, it's important to eat something and drink water to replace energy and fluid.

Sleep

Before I discuss how important sleep is and how to improve your sleep, here are two important points:

- **Everyone's 'sleep needs' are different.** So, if you hear that we need on average eight hours for adults and nine for adolescents, remember these are only averages. You might be able to manage on less, or you might function better with a bit more. You can work this out by choosing some nights when you won't be woken up by an alarm clock next morning; go to bed around 11 pm and see how long you tend to sleep for and how you feel the following day. You'll need to do this several times before you can get a true sense of whether you genuinely manage well on less than eight hours.
- **Everyone can cope on the occasional terrible night's sleep.** So, if you are lying awake and panicking about having an exam next day, don't worry because you'll almost certainly function fine. The chemical adrenaline, one of the 'stress chemicals', will carry you through. Problems only crop up after several really bad nights in a row. Also, almost everyone who has a bad night actually sleeps for longer than they thought.

How can sleep affect grades?

Although everyone's sleep needs are different and although we can function with less than the ideal, getting the best sleep you can will make a difference to how you *feel*. And you'll find it easier to produce your best work. Sleep affects concentration, for example, so if you have enough sleep you won't have to struggle so hard to focus.

Recent research has revealed much more about what happens in our brains during sleep, but there's still a lot we don't know. We used to think sleep was just for 'recharging the batteries', letting the body rest and regain energy. That's important for your brain because it uses a lot of energy (20% of the energy your body produces) and, if you're sleep deprived, it's harder for your body to get the necessary glucose from your bloodstream, so your thinking skills and decision-making will suffer. But we now know that the benefits of sleep are more complicated than that, and much more interesting.

Here are some things that research shows:

- **Our brains carry on working while we're asleep,** and they tend to work on things we struggled with during the day. Have you ever noticed that when you come back to something the next day, you often understand it better? Many experiments[13] show that going to sleep after trying to learn something has a beneficial effect on memory. Scientists believe sleep allows our brain to go over networks we were trying to create during the day, for example while trying to understand new information, and to strengthen connections between cells while discarding faulty connections.[14]

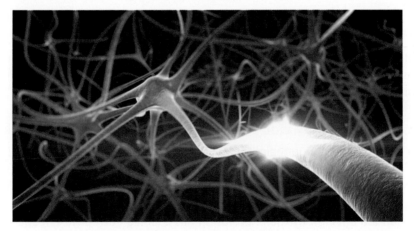

- **We have different stages of sleep, in cycles of about 90–110 minutes.** Each cycle begins with shallow sleep and moves to deeper sleep, during which it's hard to be woken up. The stages of deep sleep are important for growth and repair of damage in the body; and for moving what we learned during the day into longer term memory. At the end of each cycle, we enter REM sleep (see below).
- **The stage called Rapid Eye Movement (REM) sleep,** which usually contains most of our dreams and which is not deep sleep, seems to be important for processing traumatic events and to have a role in solving problems creatively. For example, if you were trying but failing to work something out during the day, this is when you might find a solution – as long as you woke up in time to realise and remember it! Many writers keep a notebook by their beds because they have noticed that the thoughts they have as they wake from a dream can be useful and revealing. There are well-known stories of other people coming up with very creative solutions when waking from a dream. For example, Dmitri Mendeleev created the Periodic Table in this way.
- **Our brains produce waste all the time,** which needs to be flushed away. This flushing is done by a liquid called cerebrospinal fluid. Recent research[15] suggests that during sleep brain cells shrink a little, allowing more space between them and allowing the fluid to do its job of washing away the toxins.
- **Sleep regulates certain hormones, including those that control appetite.** Poor sleep can even lead to weight gain and 'carb-cravings', with research[16] showing that people make sugar and carb-based choices the day after a bad night's sleep.
- **Lack of sleep leads to worse decision-making,** makes us more likely to be snappy with people and is strongly linked to depression and low mood.

How can you get a better night's sleep?

Most people would benefit from longer and better sleep. And even an extra 20 minutes will make a positive difference. There are several things that will help. I've split them into two: working with your body clock and understanding 'sleep hygiene'.

Working with your 'body clock' or Circadian rhythms

Have you ever noticed that you feel different at different times of day? You will have times of the day when you feel more alert and your appetite will also vary. You won't be able to measure hormone levels, but scientists know that these change during the day and night, too, affecting appetite, mood and wakefulness. These daily changes are called Circadian rhythms, and all animals are affected by them. Evolution has enabled each different species to have sleep patterns that are best and safest for that animal. The trouble is that humans changed this by inventing electricity, which means that we artificially alter our natural patterns by staying awake in hours of darkness.

How awake we feel is partly regulated by a small group of brain cells often called the 'body clock'. This responds mostly to daylight and darkness and is responsible for 'switching on' a chemical called melatonin at night, to make you feel sleepy, and switching it off again next morning. Not everyone's body clock behaves exactly the same: some people tend to be more wakeful in the mornings and are good at waking early; others work better at night. Morning people are known as 'larks' and evening people as 'owls'.

Are you a lark or an owl?

The body clock of teenagers is slightly different from that of younger children and adults. Your melatonin tends to switch on at about the same time as for adults (very roughly around 11 pm) but doesn't switch off until later in the morning than for adults. And, since you usually need more sleep than adults, on a school day you will probably not have had enough sleep and won't feel fully awake when you arrive at school. Over the week, you could end up with a pretty big sleep loss.

Look after yourself

You might think that's a perfect excuse for a weekend lie-in! Most experts say that having a moderate lie-in is a good idea, but they don't recommend staying in bed all morning, I'm afraid, as that's likely to confuse your body clock even more. But a couple of hours extra would probably be a good idea.

A better idea is to *try* to sleep slightly earlier on school nights. One way to do this is to 'trick' your brain into thinking it's later at night than it is, so your body clock switches on melatonin earlier.

There are three ways to do this – and it's important to do them all.

1. **Block daylight from your bedroom in the evening.** If your curtains don't block enough light, a blackout blind will help. Close curtains at least an hour before you want to feel sleepy. You can have a bedside light on but if your main bedroom light is very bright, I recommend turning it off: although it doesn't produce the same sort of light as daylight, low lighting will probably have the psychological effect of making you feel ready for bed.

2. **Switch off all screens – computers, laptops, tablets, phones, televisions, etc.** Sorry … all these gadgets produce light that mimics daylight – 'blue' or 'white' light-waves, and having them anywhere near your eyes can make your brain think it's daytime. If you have an electronic reading device, check whether it is 'backlit' – if it is, you need to turn it off; if it has an unlit screen, it's fine.

3. **Create a bedtime routine which your brain will recognise as signalling sleep-time.** (See below, under Sleep hygiene.)

Sleep hygiene

Sleep hygiene is the phrase to describe things we should and shouldn't do during the hour or so before we want to fall asleep. There are two reasons why good sleep hygiene will help:

 You can ensure you've done everything that encourages sleep and avoided everything that prevents it.

2 If you do the same things each evening, creating a routine, your brain will associate it with sleep, and sleep will come more easily.

To avoid in the hour before you want to feel sleepy:

- Caffeine – coffee or tea (unless decaffeinated), cola drinks
- Any exercise that raises heart rate and makes you sweat or breathe faster
- A big meal
- Loud, fast music
- Daylight – and bright lights
- Screens – computers, tablets, phones, TVs, etc.
- Arguments and stressful situations
- Talking or thinking about the things that worry you
- Alcohol – many people think alcohol might help, because they see people falling asleep while drunk. But alcohol badly disrupts sleep, so although you might *fall* asleep you will wake in the night and the toxins will have built up to make your brain and body work less well. (For more details on alcohol, see page 46.)

Good things in the hour before you want to feel sleepy:

- Get school things sorted for the morning – do this in good time, in case you realise something is missing
- Dim lighting and closed curtains
- A light snack and either a milky drink or herbal tea (anything which claims to be good for sleep and relaxation is a sensible choice)
- Gentle exercise such as yoga or stretching
- Listen to a relaxation audio
- Meditate or practise mindfulness
- Write down any worries that won't go away – then put the paper aside and stop thinking about it
- A bath or shower
- Lavender oil – in bath or on pillow
- Soft music
- Read for pleasure

Create a routine:

1 Choose a few things from the list above and decide which you will do every night, in which order.

2 Write your routine down and pin it to the wall.

3 Do it!

4 After a few nights, your brain will start to recognise the triggers for sleep.

Finally: if you've tried all these things for a couple of weeks and nothing is working, see your GP, who may be able to help in other ways. However, sleeping pills are not a long-term solution and following the advice above is a much better option.

Feed your brain

Although the brain only represents on average 2% of our weight, it uses a surprising 20% of our energy. If we don't give it enough fuel, it simply can't work properly. And food is our fuel. Although water is essential, it is not food and provides no energy.

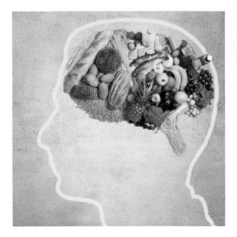

You will have heard various healthy eating messages and it can all be quite confusing. But in terms of fuelling your brain (and body) to work well during a working day and exams, the truth is not very complicated.

Here are the three most important things:

1 If you don't eat *enough*, your brain won't work so well – you'll lose concentration and find it harder to understand, learn and remember. So, don't let yourself go hungry.

2 If you don't eat enough of the *right things*, your energy levels will go up and down fast, making you feel unwell and making it harder to understand, learn and remember.

3 Although water isn't food, it's essential. If you don't keep fluid intake high enough, you will work less well.

Problems happen when you either don't eat enough food or you eat too much sugar, which makes your blood glucose levels spike and dip.

As you approach exams, this all becomes extra important. Consider:

1 Under stress, appetite changes. You may not feel like proper meals; you may rush food; and you are likely to overload with sugary carbs. These problems peak on exam days, just when a constant supply of brain fuel is most important.

2 If you don't know which foods fuel brains best, you won't know what to focus on when your appetite is poor, and you may choose sugary foods without realising their bad effect.

3 Creating an enjoyable and positive diet is one simple way to take control of health and success, with noticeable benefits.

Dieting and eating disorders

The lead-up to exams is not the right time to be restricting food intake, for the reasons I mentioned above. Your brain really does need enough of the right foods. If a doctor has said you need to lose weight or there's any medical reason why you are on a restricted diet, make sure your doctor knows that you are now doing exams. Then he or she can make sure you are getting enough of the right nutrients.

Obviously, if you have an eating disorder, being told not to restrict your food is not going to help, as it is more complicated than that. However, as you know, eating disorders are often as much about *control* as anything else, so consider how you can channel desire for control into a desire to give your brain the strongest chance to get the best exam results you are capable of.

What foods should you have in your brain-fuelling diet?

Here are some good principles:
- Avoid things with added sugar.
- Try to balance your overall diet by having a variety, making sure you have enough protein sources as well as savoury carbohydrates (see below).
- Choose the freshest food you can and generally avoid very processed foods.
- Avoid fizzy drinks.
- A yogurt at the end of a meal is a great way to finish off with some extra energy and stop you craving chocolate.
- Try to create good habits by choosing options that you actually like – so you're more likely to carry on making good choices.

Here are some great foods to include in your meals and snacks:

Good sources of protein (which will keep you full for longer): fish (especially oily fish for omega 3 content), all beans, lentils, other pulses (such as peas, chick peas), eggs, yogurt, milk and other dairy foods, nuts, chicken (not deep-fried), soya/edamame/tofu.

Good sources of carbohydrate (the ones in this list will release energy more smoothly than processed hyper-sugary carbs): vegetables, fruit (don't forget berries), dried fruit, seeds, oats and other whole grains (choose wholegrain bread, brown rice, wholegrain cereals, salads with grains and seeds in), baked potatoes (eat the skin) and sweet potatoes, avocados.

Good sources of both: dairy foods, whole grains, seeds and pulses.

You also need some oils, especially from oily fish (such as mackerel, herring and salmon – or you can take fish oil supplements) and certain seeds, such as flaxseed and pumpkin. When choosing oil for dressings, look for ones high in 'omega oils', especially omega 3.

> ### Key Point
>
> Are there 'super foods' that make brains work extra brilliantly? The science is not clear. There *are* positive findings for Brazil nuts, blueberries and oily fish, for example, but not enough evidence that they're *much* better than other perfectly nutritious foods. So, we should not eat a silly amount of one food in the belief that it will make us cleverer. As for vitamin or mineral supplements, you shouldn't need them, as most experts agree that it's best to get nutrients from your diet. An exception may be fish oils (rich in omega 3), if you don't or can't eat enough oily fish.

But just because something is good for you doesn't mean you should have far too much of it. A varied diet is always best!

Here are some ways to create meals using those foods:

Breakfast ideas – if you find it hard to eat breakfast before going to school, try to manage a yogurt and take one of the snack ideas to eat later.

- Porridge
- Cereal – avoid sugary processed ones and choose wholegrain varieties
- Beans or eggs on wholemeal toast
- Yogurt with banana or other fruit, especially blueberries
- A fruit smoothie (home-made – whizz up fruit with milk or yogurt and maybe add honey; experiment!).

Lunch ideas at school:
- Jacket potato with cheese, tuna or baked beans, plus a salad
- Chicken curry with rice and salad or fruit salad afterwards
- Fish and chips (once in a while!) and peas
- Falafel or hummus with salad and a wholegrain roll
- Lentil (or any veg) soup and a wholegrain cheese roll
- Tuna salad.

Snack ideas:
- A handful of nuts, seeds and raisins or dried apricots
- Oatcakes with cheese spread or hummus and an apple
- Carrots and avocado or hummus dip
- A yogurt and chopped up banana – maybe nuts sprinkled on top
- A tuna sandwich
- Home-made flapjack or banana cake – home-made means you know exactly what's in it; many bought biscuits and cakes contain unhealthy ingredients
- Home-made smoothie.

The effects of alcohol on learning

I'm afraid the news about alcohol and learning is bad! We don't know exactly how much alcohol it takes to have a negative effect on brain performance (and physical damage in extreme circumstances) but even a small amount will not make your brain work better – and that applies to adults, too.

Here are some things we know:

- Alcohol is a depressant – even small amounts subdue our bodies' systems and make us less reactive and less in control.
- It can make us feel relaxed and happy at first, which is why people drink it, but it *is* a mind-altering drug and it *does* alter brain function.
- It seems to take smaller amounts of alcohol for adolescent brains to be affected (based on studies in other animals[17]) and teenagers are more likely to become addicted.
- Getting *drunk* is bad for our brains, whatever our age, and harms the area of our brain important for some types of learning and long-term memory, the 'hippocampus'. This area develops fast during adolescence, which may explain why teenagers are more vulnerable to alcohol damage.
- However, don't worry about any drinking you or your friends have already done: if you stop now, there's every chance you can build up any brain networks you might have risked.

We just don't know exactly how much alcohol causes different effects in different people, but it's definitely worth protecting your developing brain by not getting drunk or using alcohol.

Your brain will thank you for looking after it with exercise, sleep and good food. You can't control everything but these are some things you can really do to take care of yourself and give yourself the best chance.

> ## Key Point
>
> - Don't go hungry. When your appetite isn't good, make sure the right ingredients are in the house so there's always something you fancy.
>
> - Take a snack box into school on exam days, so you can eat something before an exam.
>
> - Drink water. If you find plain water boring, vary it: add a slice of lemon or lime; drink it very cold; add fresh fruit juice; or drink herbal or fruit teas. Watch the sugar content of bottled water!

4

Tackling pressure head on

Danielle Brown

Danielle Brown is a double Paralympic gold medallist in archery, three times World Champion and holds all twelve world records. World number one for seven years, Danielle attributes all her success to being mentally stronger than her competitors. Being able to perform well when nervous saw her win the gold medal in London 2012. Danielle is now teaching students the strategies that elite athletes use to stay at the top of their game, helping them to perform under pressure when it matters the most. For more information on student stress levels and dealing with pressure visit www.daniellebrown.co.uk

Introduction

Exams are seriously stressful! They're an important part of your education and help determine the direction your life will take. But what if you struggle to answer the questions, your mind goes blank, or you haven't revised that topic? What if you get a really difficult paper?

Forget spiders, snakes and heights. One of our greatest fears as a race is failure. We fear not being good enough, not achieving our potential, letting those around us down and we also fear that others will see us as a failure. Does any of this sound familiar?

What is it about failure that scares us so much? Well there's a scientific reason behind it all. Unfortunately evolution hasn't quite worked in our favour here and our brains are still very primitive in lots of ways. Your brain's primary concern is to protect you from harm. To do this your subconscious focuses on threats to your wellbeing. If you know the threat is there then you can do something about it. Despite it being an incredibly clever and complex organ, the brain is unable to tell the difference between emotional trauma and physical harm. It hurts when we fail. Maybe not physically, but this is interpreted in exactly the same way as pain. That's why most people don't go into an exam wondering 'What if I ace this?' Being successful is not a threat to your wellbeing.

So all the 'what ifs', the worry and stress are just part of our natural response. However, this fear of failure can have a very negative impact on our performance. If we dwell on the consequences of underachieving the thought of failure becomes more and more terrifying. This can shake your confidence pretty badly, magnifying those nerves and making your job of taking an exam a bit more difficult.

The great news is that you can change the way you think. If you imagine your brain being a bit like a computer, all you're going to do is reprogram it. You need to strip down the negative beliefs that are currently holding you back and replace them with a much more productive way of thinking. With a bit of work you will start to look at failure completely differently! The great inventor Thomas Edison is famous for stating that he did not fail, but found a thousand ways not to make a lightbulb before he eventually got it right! So exams are really there to provide an opportunity for you to showcase your ability and all that hard work you've put in!

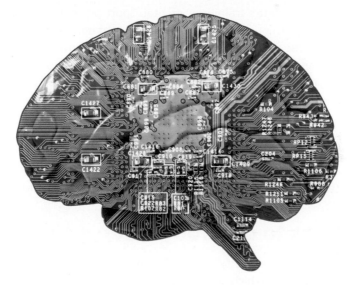

World class athletes know this. Four whole years of training goes into an Olympic performance. Can you imagine the pressure that athletes are under as they step out into the stadium and ready themselves for that performance of a lifetime? But world record breakers and gold medallists aren't plagued by questions of 'what if?' and that terrifying fear of failure. These athletes are undeniably nervous when the buzzer sounds, but confident that if they give it everything they have then the gold medal is theirs. Elite performers expect to succeed instead of trying not to fail! They go out there ready to show the world what they can do!

A large proportion of an athlete's training is mental. Sport psychology is designed to help athletes cope with these enormous pressures, channelling that nervous energy into a winning performance. Just like those world class athletes, you can learn how to successfully respond to the stress of taking an exam. This chapter uses the tried and tested techniques that help athletes power to glory, showing you how to control your nerves so you are in the best possible shape when taking an exam. These simple strategies will increase the likelihood of you achieving the grades you deserve. To successfully control those exam nerves you are going to learn:

- How and why we get nervous.
- Long and short-term coping strategies to reduce anxiety levels and build your confidence.

What happens to our body when we're nervous?

Our bodies come equipped with a pretty cool survival mechanism (the fight or flight response, discussed in chapter 2, page 24), which helps us to react to danger almost instantly – and when we are preparing for exams we often experience this fight or flight response. While we aren't facing a life or death situation we are nonetheless placed in a high pressure environment. Remember the bit about the brain not being able to tell the difference between emotional pain and physical harm? This is what's happening here and our bodies react in exactly the same way.

Some of the symptoms you might recognise include:

- Butterflies in your stomach

- Increased heart rate

- Sweaty palms

- Short, shallow breathing

- A dry mouth

- Feeling nauseous or lightheaded

- Having negative thoughts and reduced confidence

- Moodiness

- Difficulty concentrating

- Shaking

- And the one thing you really don't want happening when you're in an exam; **your mind going blank**

Apart from making you feel terrible, these symptoms can all lead to **underperformance**. Before we start delving into ways to fix this, it is important for you to understand this list of symptoms for two reasons.

1 Everybody is wired up this way so it is perfectly normal to get nervous and react like this. Your greatest sporting heroes who dominate their competition with unshakeable confidence have all experienced nerves. Jessica Ennis, poster girl for the London 2012 Olympics, admitted that she gets so nervous before competing that she could cry. So all that worry and stress about your exams is normal.

2 When we look at some of the strategies to help you cope with nerves, you will look at how to control these reactions so that they don't affect your performance in an exam. The quicker you can recognise these symptoms the sooner you can put your coping strategies into action. When I am about to compete at a high profile event my heart starts to thud in my chest and my palms go sweaty, followed very closely by a dry mouth. It is at this point that I know I am going to have to implement my coping strategies if they are going to be really effective. Everybody reacts slightly differently, so you need to work out which symptoms you display first. The next time you feel yourself getting stressed out, take a deep breath and try to pinpoint what is happening to your body. Writing it down may help.

Yet in spite of all this, **nerves are good**. The only reason you get nervous is because you want to be successful. We tend to believe that nerves are a bad thing because we experience those horrible symptoms. We don't like feeling dizzy, sick and out of control, therefore we think of nerves as being bad. But if your results didn't matter to you then you wouldn't get nervous and this is really important!

So, the aim isn't to get rid of your exam nerves completely. Pressure is good. It's motivating, it inspires you to work hard and focuses your attention. Without pressure you wouldn't bother to work at all because there would be no need to get anything done. However, it's a fine balancing act. You want a bit of pressure to help you get the most out of yourself, but you don't want the fight or flight response taking over. Too much adrenaline is going to cloud your judgement, which in most people can lead to a detrimental effect on performance. There's no need to panic when you experience those symptoms of nerves, though. Your job is to be able to control them and not allow them to hinder your performance.

Now the science bit is all done and dusted we're going to start to look at the coping strategies that will help you control these nervous reactions.

Long-term coping strategies

The long-term coping strategies all revolve around increasing your **confidence** levels. Developing a strong sense of self-belief is the most important skill you can ever master. I learned this out in Beijing at the 2008 Paralympic Games, where I had a bit of a mental meltdown the night before my competition. Yes, even Olympic champions have them sometimes! I started to doubt my ability and my thoughts became more and more negative until I'd convinced myself that my dream of becoming Paralympic champion was impossible. Our beliefs shape the way we behave and had I woken up the next day certain that I was going to lose then I probably would have done. I managed to pull myself together at the very last minute, but the realisation that we can think ourselves into failure was a lesson learned.

Confidence is just as important as intelligence or ability when it comes to taking an exam. Once you believe that you are capable of successfully taking an exam then you start to reduce the negative impact of the fear of failure. The self-doubt that plagues you begins to diminish and you stop torturing yourself over whether you're smart enough to be successful.

So what is confidence and how do we get it? Simply put, confidence is knowing that you are capable of achieving. If you believe that you have the ability to be successful in your exams then you'll be feeling a little more relaxed when that paper is put in front of you. This means that your brain won't feel as threatened, keeping the fight or flight response at a controllable level. There are four great strategies, outlined over the next few pages, that all help to build your confidence levels, changing your mindset into something more positive and productive.

Preparation

Success is wholly contingent on preparation. You need to put the work in to get the results out. Nobody gets to an Olympic Games without hours and hours of practice and taking an exam is very similar. If you can go into an exam and say to yourself 'Whatever happens today, I couldn't have worked any harder – now I just have to show the examiners how much I've learned', you can't do any more than that.

Positive past achievements

This is a great exercise to help you build your confidence levels and reduce that horrible, niggling fear of failure. Instead of dwelling on the times when things haven't quite gone well, consider all the positives. Unfortunately, we aren't very good at showering ourselves with compliments and taking pride when we have excelled at something, so you might find this task a little difficult at first. Write down your positive past achievements, listing all the times you have achieved something really great or performed under pressure. No accomplishment is too small. Check out the example and then identify your own strengths.

> **Key Point**
>
> Before you sit the exam, remind yourself just how much effort you've put in! Knowing that you've worked hard will make you feel more comfortable and confident.

Achievements I can be proud of:

- I felt I'd done really badly in my last maths exam, but I tried to answer each question and actually came away with a good grade.
- Science is my strongest subject. I'm pretty confident about this.
- I didn't think I could do my last exams. I was so nervous! But they went well and I got higher grades than I expected.
- I've practised lots of old exam papers. Now I'm more comfortable with how I should answer questions and know what the examiners expect from me.
- I've spent a long time revising each topic, working hardest at geography because I find it the most difficult.
- My parents have been really supportive and know that I've worked hard whatever the result.

Visual reminders are also really powerful so you might want to create a colourful montage for your bedroom wall, sticking up photos and certificates of your various achievements.

Key Point

Keep revisiting this, especially in those moments where you start to think you're not good enough. Use these positive past achievements to remind yourself that you do have the ability to do well in your exams.

I came away with good grades in my mock exams. Even the ones I felt went badly.

I've spent weeks revising. I know my subjects really well. Even the difficult bits don't seem so hard to understand now.

Science is my best subject! It's all about learning facts and I find it really interesting!

I AM GOING TO PASS MY EXAMS! 😊

Revising with my friends has been great. They understand how I feel and going over topics together has given me more confidence.

Challenging limiting beliefs

Every time you think the words 'I can't …' or 'What if …' you're limiting yourself, and we're all guilty of it! Negative thoughts have the power to destroy everything you've worked so hard for. If you think that you're terrible at taking exams then you probably won't be motivated to study hard. Your grades are likely to reflect this mentality, which just confirms that your original thought of being terrible at taking exams is correct. So it's time to get you thinking positively. This is where you're going to reprogram that computer in your brain.

Thoughts create feelings

Feelings create behaviour

Behaviour reinforces thoughts

As soon as a negative thought pops into your head it should start ringing alarm bells. Visualising a bright red stop sign is a really great way to challenge a negative thought.

Close your eyes now and see if you can picture one.

Once you've got that image in your mind, you need to start the process of changing your negative thought into a positive one. First, you must question your thought and ask yourself whether it's really true. This isn't an excuse for you to confirm your original thought and say 'Yes, I am rubbish at exams.' Use logic to find an answer that rejects your negative belief – no matter how impossible a situation may seem at first, there is always another way of looking at things. When you've done the questioning and found that your belief isn't true then you need to change it to a positive.

Let's go through a quick example:

1   **Negative thought:** I'm useless at taking exams. My mind goes blank every time and I can't remember anything. I know I'm going to fail.

2   **Question it:** My mind hasn't gone blank in every exam I've taken because I knew the answers in my science exams and I came away with really great grades.

3   **Turn it into a positive:** I'm not useless at taking exams. I've done it before so I know I can do it again. I've also learned some fantastic techniques that will help stop my mind from going blank in an exam ever again.

To start with you might want to write this process down, especially with the really common negative thoughts you have. That way when the thought pops into your head again you already have a response for it, allowing you to get your brain back on track much more quickly.

Imagery

The brain doesn't actually know the difference between when you imagine something and when you experience it for real. It's really not as clever as you first thought, is it? This means that you can program yourself by visualising successful outcomes or positive characteristics. I won the gold medal in London 2012 thousands of times in my mind before it happened for real. On that line, in front of that home crowd, I knew I would perform well because I'd done it so many times before.

Imagery isn't just useful in sport. You will find this technique hugely beneficial when preparing for your exams. Chances are you're already quite good at imagery if you've been picturing yourself failing your exams in spectacular fashion. But if you imagine yourself successfully taking an exam you will feel more positive, confident and relaxed when it comes to the real thing. So let's give it a go …

Key Point

If you're struggling to change your negative thoughts into positives, have a quick read through your positive past achievements. This will highlight the times you have achieved success, proving your negative thought is not right.

Close your eyes and imagine sitting at the desk with your exam paper in front of you. Feel your body relax as you pick up your pen and flick through the paper calmly. Picture yourself confidently writing your answers. What would you say to yourself in that positive state? Tying your emotions and feelings into this is more important than being able to see a really clear picture, so imagine what it feels like to be positive and relaxed while taking an exam.

Using this technique should enable you to experience that confidence on the day, when you're actually taking the exam.

Key Point

Try this at least once a day in a revision break. Five minutes is all it takes. It's important to do this if you're feeling a bit negative and are getting really worked up about your exam.

Short-term coping strategies

We've just covered four great strategies that will help you prepare for your exams. Now let's look at two really useful short-term strategies for when you get into that exam room and those nerves start to take over. Use these as soon as you recognise any of the symptoms of nerves. This will tone down the adrenaline in your system, reduce its impact and stop you from spiralling out of control.

Breathing

The easiest technique you will ever learn to help you deal with pressure is breathing! Put your hand on your stomach right now and breathe really deeply until you can feel your hand moving outwards. Try it a few more times. You feel nice and relaxed now, don't you?

Breathing deeply reduces the effect of the fight or flight response, helping you to think a little more clearly instead of reacting to the situation immediately. It's a bit like flicking a switch. Your brain sends this message to your body and it starts to reduce the amount of adrenaline in your system, allowing you to have a much more controlled response. As soon as you recognise those first symptoms of nerves, take a few moments to breathe, until you can feel them starting to recede.

Music

Music has the ability to change your state of mind and this is a fantastic technique to help control nerves! Can you remember when you had a really bad day and a certain song on the radio made you smile and put you in a better mood? You can target the particular emotional state you want to feel when you're starting to stress out just by listening to music. This activity is really easy and great fun to do in one of your revision breaks!

First, you need to identify the particular state you want to be in when you're taking an exam. Do you want to be relaxed and calm, or perhaps fired up and ready to go? Some people prefer to be

> **Key Point**
>
> Breathing deeply is a great technique to do in the middle of an exam, while you're waiting to go in or if you're getting in a bit of a state in the lead up to your exams. Just keep breathing nice and deeply until you feel yourself regaining control.

focused and others energetic and excited. If you're not sure, think back to the imagery exercise and try to recreate those positive feelings that you've been practising.

Next you need to go through your music playlist, listening to songs for about 30 seconds. Make a note of all the songs that elicit the emotion you want to feel. In this exercise you're only focusing on positive emotions. Music also has the capacity to evoke negative emotions and you really don't want to feel depressed, tense or anxious before you go into an exam so just skip past those ones.

Finally, create a playlist from the songs you've chosen. Listen to it on the way to your exam or if you start to feel yourself bubbling up with anxiety at any stage throughout your revision.

My dream was to stand on top of that podium, a gold medal around my neck. I went out there and made that dream come true because I always believed I would. I wasn't better than my competitors because I had a better technique or practised harder than they did, but because I was mentally stronger than they were and I used all of these techniques to help me. Having that unwavering self-confidence is undoubtedly the key to success and building this self-confidence will have a profound and positive impact on your results.

> ### Key Point
>
> This is a very individual activity as people react to music differently. What works for you might be different to your friends. Even if you love the same songs it could evoke different emotions and moods. There are people who find heavy metal relaxing and classical music fires them up, so there really is no right answer to this.

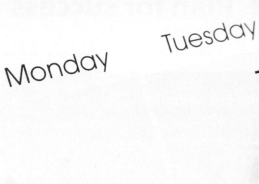

Chapter 5

M-C McInally and Eric Summers

M-C McInally and Eric Summers are experienced authors and head teachers. They have written two best-selling books on study skills and regularly speak at conferences on this subject.

Introduction

This section is about planning. It is not yet about studying. It's about getting everything *ready* for studying so that, when you do finally get down to it, you will work efficiently and effectively, making good use of your precious time to understand and remember all the topics you have to learn.

It is surprising how many people do not do this. They make the commitment to study hard but they do not prepare their study sessions carefully enough. They don't know until they start what they are going to read or write or revise. They don't have to hand the materials they are going to need. They probably aren't even sure until they finally settle down which room they are going to study in or which table they are going to sit at.

These are not *bad* students. They are sincere in wanting to study. They are prepared to work hard. They want to do well. But they are making it more difficult for themselves. They do not get as much out of the hours they spend studying as they should.

We know that planning works. Planning makes the most complicated tasks and the most forbidding challenges possible to overcome. Careful planning will ensure that your studying is systematic, well-ordered, effective, satisfying and it might even stretch to being pleasurable as well.

Setting up your space

So, first things first. Where is the best place to study? There is no right answer: the right place will be a matter of personal choice. It should be the place that best suits you. That means the place where it is easiest to study.

There is no right answer because the environment that helps one person to study may not suit another. Some people like to have one location and stick with it. It becomes associated in their minds with study. They go there and they study. The distractions are minimised. They find it easier to get started as soon as they walk through the door. Everything is familiar and everything says to them, 'This is where I study and that is why I am here.'

Others like variety. They find that moving from one location to another is refreshing. It re-energises them for another study session. This tends to be the pattern in school. The place of study moves from one location to another throughout the day, stopping and starting, changing rooms and teachers as well. These interruptions may actually help your learning (see pages 107–108).

But, after school, you should be able to set up your study space or spaces in the way you like. To help you do this part of your planning, you might find it helpful to watch what other people do. Do you have an older brother or sister, perhaps one who is at college or university? Ask them what they do. Ask your teacher. Maybe you could get some inspiration from famous and successful people.

Two centuries ago standing desks were quite common. One Prime Minister always worked in the same room, standing at his high desk. He believed it was better for his back than sitting and it also helped him concentrate. He was less likely to put his head down and fall asleep!

A very successful modern novelist, who admittedly has earned enough money to have a big house, has three study locations. In the morning she writes in one room, in the afternoon she moves to a second room and, in the evening, when her family is home, the television is on and things are generally much less quiet, she retreats to her third location which is in the attic. She probably liked changing classrooms when at school!

Several authors like having a writing hut in the garden. They get out of the house, walk the few steps to their shed, which they have all set up with everything they need, close the door and work away undisturbed. Roald Dahl worked this way and so too did Charles Dickens later in his career.

All these people gave thought to what was best for them and you must do the same. Your choices will probably be limited (until you become rich and famous), but there will still be options and you should consider each carefully, perhaps after trying out the various possibilities.[18]

School

When the final bell goes, most pupils cannot wait to get out of the school. But think about it. The school is quickly going to become quiet. All you need for studying is going to be to hand. The school library will be warm, with internet connections if you have to check information online. You could get a really good hour's work done before going home. It's worth considering, unless of course you have to catch a bus.

Local library

Another possibility might be the local library. The number of other people you see there might surprise you. There could be university students, also preparing for exams. There might be senior citizens, retired and now with the freedom to pursue their own interests. And there could be you, getting in another hour or two of good learning.

Your bedroom

Not everyone has his or her own bedroom. But, if you are lucky enough to have your own room, then this is likely to be your preferred location for studying. You can set it up exactly as you want it (and we'll discuss doing that shortly) and it will give you the privacy, the peace and the quiet to get really focused and concentrate on your studies. Your bedroom might still be the best place even if you do share. Perhaps you can negotiate with your siblings the times when you can have it to yourself, when you can put a 'Do not disturb' sign on the door.

Another room in your house

Can you claim an area that could be set up as a dedicated study? It could be a spare room, a dining room, or it might be a bit of the kitchen that has to double as a study area. You will still be able to carve out an area that is yours, where you have a table or desk, a chair, a bookcase and a wi-fi connection.

The sitting room

The reality is that many modern houses do not have spare rooms and often you have to share the accommodation. There may be only one room available and everyone else expects to use it as well. The television may be on and there might be much coming and going. This is where families must try to pull together. Ask if you can have peace and quiet for just one hour. Or time your big study sessions when you know other family members will be out. Or even try studying with earphones on, not to listen to music but to cut out the noise. This will not be easy but many famous people responded to the challenge of their circumstances when they were young. You can too.

Someone else's house

This can be very good, but you and your friend have to know each other well and be very disciplined. You can support each other, ask each other questions, explain tricky maths problems to each other. You are equally likely to distract each other, and then persuade yourselves that you spent a good evening studying. You did not! And you should not delude yourself that you did. Good studying is about being honest with yourself. So, do the business first. Agree that you are going to work, *really* work, for an hour or two hours or whatever. Do just that. *Then* relax and do the other things.

Whichever place you settle on, you must then arrange it to give you the maximum benefit. So much time can be wasted hunting for lost notes, sharpening pencils, spilling coffee and responding to texts. The old adage of a place for everything and everything in its place was never more valid than for a study area. A desk that looks like this:

> ### Key Point
>
> The best place for you may well be a combination of places – school, public library and your own bedroom for example. Experiment, but do so well before the heat is really turned up and the pressure of exams becomes intense. Decide on what is to be your study zone(s) and then stick to it.

may work for an eccentric genius, but you will benefit from a desk like this:

Here is what you need:

1 **A desk or table:** You will of course be tempted to lounge in a comfortable chair or even lie on your bed to read and write. But it is a table or desk you really need. It provides a good writing surface and a place to spread out your books and notes. Sitting at a desk is also better for your posture than slouching in the depths of an armchair. As you study, you should want to look after your health as well.

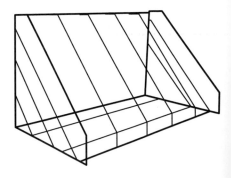

2 **A bookcase or shelf:** We'll discuss later how to take and keep notes (pages 87–96). For now you need to remember that all the notes in the world are no use to you if you can't quickly lay your hands on them. It is the same with textbooks. Ideally you don't even want to get out of your chair to select the book you need. So, place your folders and key books properly on a shelf with everything to do with History together, everything to do with English together, and so on. Folders, you will have noticed, easily become untidy and fall over. It's worth investing in a rack to keep them upright. The one pictured here costs less than £10·00.

3 **A computer:** It's the 21st century. We can't pretend you don't need a computer of some sort. This of course might be a tablet or iPad. For taking electronic notes, word processing essays and creating presentations a computer is now less of a luxury and more of an essential. If you do not have one, you should make full use of the equipment in the school library when it is open.

4 **Access to the internet:** Using the school or your local library will also be necessary if you don't have an internet connection at home. The internet does not replace books but it is an essential complement. You need to be able to surf the web … and we're not talking here about watching YouTube and updating Facebook!

5 **A notepad:** For writing notes! Yes, you still have to do that. Don't use old jotters or scraps of paper. Get a decent lined pad and a blank pad, and one with graph paper as well if you are studying mathematical or technical subjects.

6 **Pens, pencils, erasers, highlighters:** You need a good supply right beside you. Do not discover in the middle of a study session that they are missing or not working.

7 **Paperclips and a stapler:** These simple tools can impose order on chaos. Keep them handy, use them, and don't forget to have a box of staples ready for when the stapler runs out.

8 **Any specialist equipment:** Depending on what you are studying, there may be other pieces of equipment that you will require. Establish and acquire exactly what you need.

So, you are all set up. You know where you are going to study, you're organised, you have all the tools for the job and you're ready to go. Well, not quite! There are a few more things to think about first.

Creating schedules and tracking progress

All big projects have to be 'done right'. For instance, in engineering, there is no point in building an impressive tunnel that collapses a few years later. Nor would it work simply to say we will have it built by such and such a date and hope it happens on time. And there would be very little point in pressing on with the digging if mistakes at an earlier stage mean the tunnel is heading in the wrong direction. All these real engineering concerns contain lessons for the student preparing for exams. They give us three golden rules for studying:

1 It is about quality not quantity.

2 The work has to be done regularly according to a schedule.

3 There must be frequent checks to confirm that learning is definitely taking place and the schedule is being adhered to.

Following these rules will ensure your studying is worthwhile and that you will pass your exams (and that the tunnel will not cave in!). So, let's look at each of the rules in turn.

1 Quality not quantity

This is not an invitation to neglect your studies – you have to put the hours in. But how many hours? Well, it depends on the individual and how long it takes that person to master what they are trying to learn.

The point here is that you do not achieve mastery by simply sitting in a library for hours. That in itself is just a waste of time, unless you really are learning. The chances are you will not be: your mind will be wandering, you will be allowing yourself to be distracted, you will be deluding yourself that you are studying.

Never forget this: **10 minutes of truly focused studying is better than an hour of daydreaming.**

2 Creating a schedule

Stage 1: establishing how much time you have available

You do not have 24 hours available every day. You have to sleep, you have to eat, you might have to spend time travelling and you do need time to spend with family and friends.

In this stage we are seeking to identify what time we have for studying, making sure it is enough, and then deciding when it should take place.

Here is an example which illustrates that something will have to be cut to get a decent number of hours for studying in the course of a week:

Category	Activity	Frequency	Hours involved			
Essential	Sleeping	Daily × 8 hours	56			
	Eating	Daily × 3 hours	21			
	Travel	5 days × 1 hour	5			
	Personal care	Daily × 1 hour	7			
	At school	5 days × 6 hours	30			
Very desirable	Socialising	3 days × 3 hours	9			
	Training & playing (in travelling)	2 days × 3 hours	6			
	Drama club	1 day × 2 hours	2			
Could be reduced	Watching TV & online	Daily × 3	21			
	Lazing about	7 days × 2 hours	14			
					Total hours in the week	168
		Time used	171		Time left for studying	−3
					Target is 12	12

Plan for success

Now, you have a go at completing this blank version, putting in the activities that you participate in:

Category	Activity	Frequency	Hours Involved			
Essential						
Very desirable						
Could be reduced						
					Total hours in the week	168
		Time used			Time left for studying	
					Target is 12	12

If you are honest with yourself when doing this exercise, you might find it quite hard to hit the target figure of 12 hours. But that is what you must do. As we move on to constructing a study timetable you need to have at least 12 hours available for private study. That is two hours a night for six days, with one day off, or it could be two days off if you put in some extra time on another night. We can see what that might look like in stage 3. But before that we have ....

Stage 2: recording key dates and deadlines

Your school or individual teachers may issue you with these. Go looking for them if they don't. What you require are:

- The dates of your final exams.
- The dates of any prelim/mock exams.
- The dates of any unit or interim tests that you have to pass to be allowed to continue.
- The pattern of homework issue for all your subjects. This might be difficult. Some teachers are helpful. They issue a homework exercise on Thursdays, require it to be handed in on Monday, return it on the following Thursday and issue a new one for the next Monday. You know where you are with them. Others are more erratic or informal in issuing homework. It is unfair of these teachers to give you a major piece of work for the following day. That will disrupt your study schedule. If any teacher does this – and it is to be hoped none does – you or several pupils in the class should discuss the matter with him or her.
- Holiday dates.

Put these dates into a planner for the year, so that you can see them at a glance. Armed with this information you are now ready to create your weekly timetable or schedule.

Stage 3: building a weekly timetable

Now you can start to pull everything together in your own personalised schedule. You want to be doing the right things at the right time throughout the school session, using the schedule to keep yourself on track.

Look at this example.

Week beginning: 21 February				*Weekly Rating*			Good-On Track	Minor Concerns	Action Required
	Mon	Tues	Wed	Thurs	Fri	Sat	Sun	*Homework due this week*		
00-01.00										
01.00-02.00										
02.00-03.00										
03.00-04.00										
04.00-05.00										
05.00-06.00										
06.00-07.00								*Test this week*		
07.00-08.00										
08.00-09.00										
09.00-10.00										
10.00-11.00										
11.00-12.00								*Key Topics for revision*		
12.00-13.00								*Subject*	*Topic*	*L*
13.00-14.00										
14.00-15.00										
15.00-16.00										
16.00-17.00										
17.00-18.00										
18.00-19.00										
19.00-20.00										
20.00-21.00										
21.00-22.00										
22.00-23.00										
23.00-00.00										
Prelims Dates	**15-20 January**			*Finals:*	**1-20 May**		Milestone Review	Yes/No		

A schedule such as this should be filled in by you every week. Let's look at each element in turn.

- The top row identifies the week and then a weekly rating which you would complete at the end of the week. Ring **Good**, **Minor Concerns** or **Action Required** to indicate how you well you feel you have kept to the schedule.

- Down the left hand column are the hours in the day, while across the top on the left hand side are the days of the week. You need to shade in each cell for every day in the week. In this example:
  - Blue shows SLEEP – eight hours a night with some extra time at the weekend.
  - Green shows time for GETTING WASHED and DRESSED, EATING, TRAVEL, etc.
  - Yellow is TIME IN SCHOOL, including lunch breaks.
  - Orange is for a particular LEISURE ACTIVITY. It could be training and playing a sport, or taking part in amateur dramatics, or something completely different. A hobby of some sort.
  - Purple is SOCIALISING, WATCHING TV or perhaps ON THE COMPUTER. It is essentially down time, relaxation time.
  - Bright red is STUDY and in this case it amounts to 12 hours exactly.
- The right hand side of the schedule is just as important. At the start of the week, or perhaps on Sunday night, write down the homework that will be due over the next five days, any tests that are coming up, and then, below that section, list each subject that you are studying and the particular topic that you plan to concentrate on in this particular week and how many minutes you intend spending on it. (The L column will be explained a little later (page 105).
- This critical analysis of the work you have to do is part of the secret to achieving quality studying. Using a schedule will mean that when you settle down to work you will know exactly what you want to learn and the setting of a number of minutes to each task will ensure that each subject is given its fair share of your study time. You are going to be efficient as well as effective.
- Along the bottom of the schedule are very clear reminders of when your prelims/mocks and final exams are, and then a place for a milestone review (see 3 below).

A few more points to bear in mind about scheduling:
- The above example must be customised to suit *your* interests, commitments and family arrangements.
- It should be used in conjunction with a year planner.
- It must be maintained. It must be filled in and reviewed every week. That should not take long, but it must be done if you are going to derive any benefit.
- So, there is a case for numbering the weeks as well as including the date.
- It is probably most convenient to set up the schedule on a computer. Then you can easily make however many copies you need, with the recurring features of the week, like SLEEP and SCHOOL, remaining fixed, and other elements being easily adjusted on an ongoing basis.

Plan for success

Now have a go with this blank version. Fill it in with your details.

Week beginning:				Weekly Rating			Good-On Track	Minor Concerns	Action Required
	Mon	Tues	Wed	Thurs	Fri	Sat	Sun	Homework due this week	
00-01.00									
01.00-02.00									
02.00-03.00									
03.00-04.00									
04.00-05.00									
05.00-06.00									
06.00-07.00								Test this week	
07.00-08.00									
08.00-09.00									
09.00-10.00									
10.00-11.00									
11.00-12.00								Key Topics for revision	
12.00-13.00								Subject	Topic	L
13.00-14.00									
14.00-15.00									
15.00-16.00									
16.00-17.00									
17.00-18.00									
18.00-19.00									
19.00-20.00									
20.00-21.00									
21.00-22.00									
22.00-23.00									
23.00-00.00									
Prelims Dates				Finals:				Milestone Review	Yes/No	

3 Monitoring a schedule

Big engineering projects, or a company developing a new product, will not only have a date for final completion but will have important 'milestones' in place as part of their schedule. These are like checkpoints which help monitor whether each part of the main project is being completed satisfactorily and on time. You need milestones as well, so that you can track whether your studying is actually delivering the knowledge and understanding that you will need to pass your exam.

The key dates we recorded above are part of this process. Ongoing tests, exercises marked and returned by the teacher and mock/preliminary exams will tell you how you are doing. Your aim is to be at your best for the final exam. Early on in any course you might not do so well. It usually takes time to get your head round new and difficult concepts and into the way of writing or problem solving required by any particular subject. But you should be looking to make progress, to be steadily improving and growing in confidence. If you are not meeting your milestones, you will have to review your study schedule. You should certainly discuss it with your teacher and check that you are working on the right things to improve (See chapter 7).

But even if your marks suggest you are doing okay, it is still worthwhile sitting down regularly to review your study schedule. Once a fortnight would be appropriate. Answer the following questions honestly:

- Am I getting eight hours of good sleep every night?
- Am I eating well or have I gone back to consuming junk food?
- Is my desk/table/study-bedroom still tidy with all my study materials where they should be?
- Are my folders in place and up to date with all my notes properly filed?
- Am I keeping to my study slots conscientiously?
- Has it been *quality* studying or have I just filled up the hours? Your answer to this question requires brutal honesty!
- Have I been completing school assignments on time? Have I been meeting deadlines, in other words?

Answering the above questions is you having a conversation with yourself and can be as private as you want to make it. However, when the truthful answer is 'No', because you know very well that you have not been keeping to some aspect of the schedule, then 'No' is the answer you give yourself.

And then you do something about it! You do some rescheduling. Or you re-dedicate yourself to *quality* studying. Or you seek help.

You do not just leave it. Because that means you will continue to drift from the schedule and things will get worse. You will know you let yourself down. So don't!

Refer back now to the weekly schedule and to the bottom line and the section marked Milestone Review. The suggestion we have just made is that this should take place once a fortnight. Circle 'Yes' if this is a milestone week and, if it is, ask yourself the key monitoring questions and then write one sentence in the box summing up how you are doing. Actually writing down your assessment matters. Keeping it in your head is all very well, but putting it down on paper, or typing it in on the computer, forces you to confront your failings, as you must. If you are doing well, give yourself a congratulatory comment because you will deserve it.

This chapter has been about planning. We have spent time on it because good planning produces rewards. There is no great secret in all the above. It's the doing of it that can be difficult. That's what the next chapter is about.

To finish this chapter, here is how Benjamin Franklin, one of the greatest figures in American history, tried to spend his day, more than 250 years ago:[19]

SCHEME.

	Hours.	
MORNING. The *Question*. What good shall I do this day ?	5 6 7	Rise, wash, and address *Powerful Goodness !* Con-trive day's bussiness, and take the resolution of the day ; prosecute the present study, and breakfast.
	8 9 10 11	Work.
NOON.	12 1	Read, or look over my accounts, and dine.
AFTERNOON.	2 3 4 5	Work.
EVENING. The *Question*. What good have I done to-day ?	6 7 8 9	Put things in their places, Supper, Music or diversion, or conversa-tion. Examination of the day.
Night	10 11 12 1 2 3 4	Sleep.

If he believed in scheduling, perhaps you should as well.

Chapter 6

Take responsibility for your own learning

Take responsibility for your own learning

M-C McInally and Eric Summers

M-C McInally and Eric Summers are experienced authors and head teachers. They have written two best-selling books on Study Skills and regularly speak at conferences on this subject.

Introduction

In September 2014 a referendum took place to decide whether Scotland should separate itself from the rest of the United Kingdom. The background to this and its outcome (Scotland stayed!) need not concern us here. What is of interest is that 16- and 17-year-olds were allowed to vote for the first time in the UK.

There were those who were unhappy about this. They thought young people were too immature to vote responsibly. But Scotland's 16- and 17-year-olds clearly showed that this was not the case. No commentator has suggested that these young Scots did anything other than treat the democratic process with the greatest respect. They took responsibility for learning about the referendum, thought about it, and then voted in massive numbers.

This chapter is about taking a similar approach to your learning in school. Accept that it is a privilege to have the opportunity to acquire knowledge, skills and understanding about the world and everything within it, because for centuries such education was denied to most people and still is in many parts of the world.

But to make the most of this opportunity, you have to accept the responsibility of being in charge of your own learning. It is not someone else's job to learn 'stuff' for you. A teacher can tell you, show you, point you in the right direction, but if you do not understand that it is your business to actually do the learning, you will get little out of your time in school and you will be badly prepared for later in life.

Along with the right to go to school comes the responsibility to learn.

Here is how you take responsibility for your own learning. You make sure that you:

* have the right mindset
* understand why learning to study independently is important
* apply appropriate study skills.

Mindset

This is quite a simple idea. Your attitude to studying, and to work and life generally, matters. If you approach a task reluctantly and feel negatively about it, it is unlikely to go well. If you are positive and get on with it, it will be an altogether more satisfactory experience. This is just common sense and your granny could have told you as much.

However, Professor Carol Dweck of Stanford University has done a lot of work in this field,[20] confirming what many have always known, but also exploring *why* people adopt a certain mindset and the *consequences* of their choice.

Fixed mindset

Many people have a **fixed** mindset. They fear failure and avoid challenges. If they do not pass a test, they find plenty of excuses but will be unwilling to confront head on the simple fact that they did not work hard enough. They might well be scared of working hard, since this is something intelligent people shouldn't have to do. They don't want to appear hard working because that would mean admitting they are not intelligent.

Of course this is nonsense, but people may think this way because parents and teachers have praised them too much when they were young, telling them so often that they were clever or good at something, that they find it a shock when, as they get older, they realise some things are actually quite hard and an adult won't always be there to praise them or even to do it for them.

Whether it is at age 12 or age 17 that you realise that success does not always come easily, you will find a fixed mindset crippling. It will tell you to sidestep the challenge, to settle for the easy life, perhaps even to give up altogether. And what a shame that would be!

Growth mindset

The alternative is to cultivate a **growth** mindset. If you can build this sort of attitude it will mean that you look positively on challenges. You will not fear failure but see it as an opportunity to discover what you have to work harder at.

> ### Key Point
>
> Fixed mindsets can create problems not just in the classroom. Many young footballers, who seem to be very good at age eight, playing with just a few others in the primary school playground, get an unpleasant surprise when they arrive at a big secondary school and discover there are others just as good as, and maybe better than they are. The keen footballer gets the same shock when they try to turn professional. They are not special after all!

You won't avoid people who seem to be better than you. You will observe what they do and practise so that you can perform skills as they do. You will understand that while there are undoubtedly very clever and gifted people in the world, they all also work very hard at being good at what they do. This includes the pupils who win prizes at school. They may not admit it but, as well as being clever anyway, they almost certainly study as much as anyone in the building.

If you have this growth mindset you will get more satisfaction from success because, having worked hard, you will have earned it. From every failure you will emerge not depressed but pleased that you have learned something. You will not give up. You will get there. And, what is more, you will be a happier person.

Granny just knew all the above was true. Carol Dweck, by conducting rigorous research, has proved it.

So, think about mindset. Discuss it with your teachers and parents/carers. Even if it does not come naturally to you, you can work at it and move yourself from a fixed to a growth outlook on life. It's a no-brainer. Don't be fixed, go for growth. It might be the most important thing you do ... ever!

The importance of independent study

If you are developing a growth mindset, you will also be on the road to understanding what independent study is all about and why it matters. You are studying in order to pass exams, of course you are. But then what?

Why do you take driving lessons? In order to pass the driving test. Then what? Then you can drive a car on your own. You can drive independently.

What your teachers want, and what you should want for yourself, is for you to be able to study on your own, independently, and, even more importantly, after the exams have all been passed, to make use of what you have learned to earn a living, to make a contribution to society and to the economy, to derive personal satisfaction from having knowledge and skills, to be able to keep yourself up to date and still learning for the rest of your life ... without anyone having to sit beside you.

So, having accepted the responsibility of being in charge of your own learning and armed with a growth mindset, your aim must be to become an independent learner. This means:

- you listen to your teacher because, at this stage anyway, he or she knows more than you do;
- you do your assignments because they will reinforce the knowledge and understanding you are seeking to acquire.

But it also means:

- you do not wait to be told to do something when you are perfectly capable of getting on with it on your own;
- you constantly look for connections (see *Study skills* below);
- you come up with your own ideas – for an essay, a project, or whatever;

- you extend your knowledge by seeking out additional information online and in the library;
- you talk about what you are studying;
- you carry on studying at home if for some reason you have to be absent from school;
- you see what you are studying as interesting (*because it is* and realising this is part of having a growth mindset!);
- you look beyond the exams; you see that there is a greater purpose than passing them, namely to become an educated adult who will derive pleasure and satisfaction from learning throughout life and who will play a full part in the community and country in which you live.

And you know, if you become an independent learner as described, you will find the exams so much easier. You will not go into the exam room worrying that you might forget something you tried to memorise the night before; you will go through the door quietly confident because, quite simply, you know your stuff. How good is that?

Study skills

Pay attention in class

Many students think being in class is something different from studying. Class is just class. You have to be there. Studying is what you do, or maybe don't do, afterwards. This is crazy thinking.

In class you have the teacher's time. The teacher knows the subject and knows what is required to pass the exam. Why make life harder for yourself by not **listening carefully** to the expert when you have the chance?

How much easier that is than struggling to understand a difficult concept when you are on your own and the expert is not there to help you.

The truth is that many students do not listen well. And even more switch off after the teacher has been talking for more than 15 minutes. Teachers have to take some of the blame here. They often talk for too long and that makes it difficult for their students to keep concentrating. However, that is a matter for a book for teachers.

But here is some research that should be of interest to both teachers and students. A few years ago, using unobtrusive cameras and microphones, a New Zealand researcher investigated how learning actually takes place in a classroom.[21] Cameras showed how the pupils were reacting as the teacher spoke and the microphones picked up student discussion as well as the whispered conversations that were going on. What did this research reveal?

First, it showed that peer relationships in the classroom are very important. Some pupils were intimidated by stronger personalities. When a particular pupil was talking nonsense he or she was sometimes not challenged. Some pupils were very unpleasant to each other, using derogatory language that damaged the learning atmosphere.

But the most serious conclusion from the research was that many pupils were learning as much from their fellow pupils as from the teacher! The teacher perhaps thought that she had explained things very clearly, but as soon as her presentation stopped and the pupils were asked to get on with a piece of work on their own or in a group, many pupils turned to their neighbour to ask what they were to do, or to check a fact, or to clarify their understanding of the topic being studied.

Pupils helping each other can be a very powerful learning experience, but this research was rather alarming. Often the pupils remembered what their classmates told them better than what the teacher had said. Even more seriously, **what the pupil neighbour told them was often wrong!**

Take responsibility for your own learning

This is very concerning. Not only does it mean that pupils do not pay sufficient attention to the teacher when she is talking and therefore do not fully grasp important topics. It means that what they are learning is not correct.

The time to learn something is when you first hear about it – and that is usually when the teacher is explaining it. If you only half 'get it', which is what happens if you are not giving the teacher your full attention, your understanding will be confused.

Worse still is if you think you have 'got it' because your neighbour told you. You may then have learned false information and, if you are going to pass exams, you are going to have to unlearn it. You are going to have to break the new connection in your brain and do some re-programming. That is often very hard to do.

This New Zealand research is tremendously important. Keep it mind as you continue your studies and give the teacher your full attention.

Students can help themselves by asking questions. Don't wait till the teacher asks you. Listen carefully to what is being said, think about it and then ask, unprompted, a sensible question. The teacher will be delighted and, in asking it, you will be forcing yourself to concentrate. The answer you get will increase your understanding of the subject and make it easier to remember. It will turbo-charge your next private study session.

Go on try it. Ask a question. You will be amazed the impact it has on both you and the teacher.

Get your materials organised

We talked in chapter 5 about having a shelf or bookcase for your books and folders. Folders are a crucial part of your study equipment, but they can easily get into a terrible mess and that will not help you at all.

Folders should be labelled and *only* contain the notes they are supposed to have in them. An expanding concertina file can be very useful. It is the equivalent of having half a dozen standard folders lying loose.

Ring binders need to have dividers so that different sections of a course or particular topics can be easily accessed. It is extraordinary how some students abuse their ring binders. Notes are missing, stuck in upside down, or in the wrong order, often unpunched. Here is what you want:

A folder or binder for each subject is a good idea.

If you have all the notes for all your subjects filed correctly in a row of binders sitting near your table or desk then you will be making a very good start to effective studying. Remember, disorganisation creeps up on you. Notes need to be correctly marked and filed every night. Do that and you will save yourself time in the long run and much angst later on.

Always know what you are trying to learn

It is a golden rule to be clear *before* the study session begins what you intend practising, memorising, writing or what problems you are going to tackle. Imagine you are going to work for two hours in the school library. Walk through the door already knowing *exactly* what you are going to work on, with the books and notes you will require already in your hand along with all pens, pencils, calculators, etc., that you will need.

The study session in your schedule is for studying, not for thinking about studying or preparing for studying, but for actually doing the business itself.

Get rid of distractions

You can't multi-task. Don't kid yourself that you can do two things at the same time. You can't.

Scientists have shown convincingly that people who appear to be doing several things all at once are actually rapidly moving their concentration back and forward between different tasks and that they are paying a price. Every time they swap their attention they have to re-focus. That takes time and it is inefficient and confusing. We are better to concentrate on one thing at a time, do it properly, and then move on to the next task.

This means that a basic study skill is to switch off distractions. This can be painful. Teenagers nowadays probably find switching off the television not too difficult, but switching off the phone and internet can cause real agony. That of course is illustrating the point.

As mentioned earlier, there are particular difficulties if you have to study in a room shared with other people. Earphones will block out some noise, even if they are not plugged into any music.

It is true, however, that rather than being a distraction music might actually help studying. An honest evaluation is required here. Is the music really helping you and not distracting you? If it's the latter switch it off. If it's the former make sure it continues to support and not undermine your studying. The volume should be low and the music itself should be smooth and relaxing, not jagged and disruptive.

Maintain focus

Even with the external distractions switched off, it can be very difficult to keep your mind focused. What we can do is really concentrate for short bursts of time and then train ourselves to makes these periods a bit longer.

Try this.

- Identify a short very specific piece of work to learn, say memorising a couple of verses of a poem.
- Set a timer for 10 minutes.
- Wipe out all other thoughts and get these verses memorised.
- Stop when the timer goes and give yourself a two minute break, thinking about anything you like.
- Go again for another 10 minutes.

How did you get on? If the answer is badly, try the exercise with just five minute focus periods. If you stick with this approach you will find that for relatively short periods of time, if there are no distractions, you can empty your mind of all the extraneous stuff and really concentrate. With practice you should be able to get the 10 minutes up to half an hour. But, after 30 minutes you really should have a break, so that the crazy bit of your brain can jump about for a bit before being put back in its box.

You should work towards a two-hour study session that looks something like this:

- Everything ready to go; books and other materials in their place; phone and television switched off; what is to be learned clearly identified.
- 30 minutes: intense concentrated study.
- 3 minutes: break, drink of water, a few silly thoughts.
- 30 minutes: intense concentrated study.
- 3 minutes: break.
- 30 minutes: intense concentrated study.
- 3 minutes: break.
- 20 minutes: concentrated study (you'll be tiring now).
- Finish: reflect on what you've learned; turn it over in your mind as you put your books and papers away.
- Relax and feel good about yourself. You will have made significant progress.

Thinking about it

Another very effective study technique is to think about your subject, rather than just trying to remember key facts. Here are four ways to make yourself think.

1 Extend what you have been told in class or read in your textbook by doing a little extra research. Suppose you have been learning about gravity. Take five minutes to check out a bit more of Newton's life on Wikipedia.

2 Tell someone at home, in your own words, what you have learned today at school. That's a quick way of finding out whether you really were listening and understood what you were told.

3 Discuss, argue, disagree with a fellow student about what you were learning in a particular class. Imagine the class has been reading *Hamlet.* Try disagreeing with the teacher's interpretation and convincing a friend that you are right and the teacher is wrong. Do this and you and your friend will be helping each other think, remember and understand.

4 Make connections! This is a very good way of fixing knowledge in your brain. Link new stuff to what you already know, perhaps from another class. For example, don't just read Wilfred Owen's poetry in the English class. Make connections with what you know about the First World War from the History class. Making connections exercises and strengthens the brain.

Revise from the beginning

Get started revising your work as soon as possible. Good revision doesn't take place at the end of a course. Good revision begins on day one of the course because it is practice that makes perfect. This is so important that we have devoted the next chapter to it.

Note-taking

This is a crucial study skill because:

* it forces you to read, listen and watch more carefully;
* it encourages you to get to the key information;
* it helps you remember important ideas;
* it gives you a resource to return to for revision purposes.

In other words, note-taking helps you become **engaged in your own learning,** helping you to become an **independent learner**.

Unfortunately many students make some elementary mistakes in note-taking:

* They simply copy out chunks of books or cut and paste from the internet without making the effort to put the information into their own words.
* They do not think about the information as they note it down.
* They do not maintain their notes well and fail to file them properly.
* They go crazy with highlighter pens, illuminating everything except themselves.
* They do not review their notes, going back to add to them and, perhaps, in the light of greater knowledge, altering them.

Take responsibility for your own learning

The truth is that note-taking is hard work. You have to concentrate and you are pretty much on your own as you do it. But the rewards are great. You will understand so much better and remember so much more if you have made your own notes.

So, it is worth investing some time in thinking about how you are going to take notes. You have a range of options, so you want to choose the approach that suits you best.

Let's look at some examples. Here is a page about stars, taken from a book called *Bang!* [22]

The stars are remote. To try to give their distances in miles or kilometres would be as clumsy as giving the distance between London and New York in inches, but fortunately there is a better unit to hand. Light does not travel instantaneously; it flashes along at the rate of 186,000 miles per second (300,000 kilometres per second), so that in one year it covers nearly 6 thousand billion miles (9.6 thousand billion kilometres). This is what has become known as the light-year (note that it is a unit of distance and not time). The nearest star beyond the Sun is just over 4 light-years away, while the most remote objects so far recorded are over 12 billion light-years from us. Seen across such vast distances, the stars shine merely as tiny points of light. Appearances are deceptive; many of the stars visible on any clear night are not only much more luminous than the Sun, but also much larger. For example, Betelgeux in the constellation of Orion, over 300 light-years away, is vast. Its globe could contain the entire orbit of the Earth round the Sun. Some features have been detected on its surface, but only the Sun is near enough to be studied in real detail – and much of our knowledge of the stars in general depends upon what we have learned from studying our own neighbourhood star. Fortunately, the Sun is a very normal star, neither particularly powerful nor particularly feeble, and certainly not as variable as many. Astronomers rank it as a dwarf, but in fact it seems to be slightly more massive than the average – and giant stars such as Betelgeux are much less numerous than the dwarfs. We can also gain a great deal of understanding by looking at the colours of the stars. Just as we talk of objects being red- or white-hot, with white-hot objects being hotter than red-hot ones, so the colours of the stars reflect their temperatures. Betelgeux, for example, appears red because it is cooler than our own Sun, whereas Rigel – the other bright star in Orion – is blue-white and is much hotter than our own, yellow Sun, which is intermediate in temperature as well as in size.

How might you go about taking notes, so that you will understand and remember the key information?

In this first example, the student has written on the page, underlining some key words (a highlighter might have been used), drawn connectors to link information and added a little in the margin. You can do this if you own the book or if you are writing on a hand out.

The stars are remote. To try to give their distances in miles or kilometres would be as clumsy as giving the distance between London and New York in inches, but fortunately there is a better unit to hand. Light does not travel instantaneously; it flashes along at the rate of 186,000 miles per second (300,000 kilometres per second), so that in one year it covers nearly 6 thousand billion miles (9.6 thousand billion kilometres). This is what has become known as the light-year (note that it is a unit of distance and not time). The nearest star beyond the Sun is just over 4 light-years away, while the most remote objects so far recorded are over 12 billion light-years from us. Seen across such vast distances, the stars shine merely as tiny points of light. Appearances are deceptive; many of the stars visible on any clear night are not only much more luminous than the Sun, but also much larger. For example, Betelgeux in the constellation of Orion, over 300 light-years away, is vast. Its globe could contain the entire orbit of the Earth round the Sun. Some features have been detected on its surface, but only the Sun is near enough to be studied in real detail – and much of our knowledge of the stars in general depends upon what we have learned from studying our own neighbourhood star. Fortunately, the Sun is a very normal star, neither particularly powerful nor particularly feeble, and certainly not as variable as many. Astronomers rank it as a dwarf, but in fact it seems to be slightly more massive than the average – and giant stars such as Betelgeux are much less numerous than the dwarfs. We can also gain a great deal of understanding by looking at the colours of the stars. Just as we talk of objects being red- or white-hot, with white-hot objects being hotter than red-hot ones, so the colours of the stars reflect their temperatures. Betelgeux, for example, appears red because it is cooler than our own Sun, whereas Rigel – the other bright star in Orion – is blue-white and is much hotter than our own, yellow Sun, which is intermediate in temperature as well as in size.

Margin notes: Distance light travels in a year

Margin notes: Giant star, cooler than sun

In the next example the student has converted the key information into bullet points.

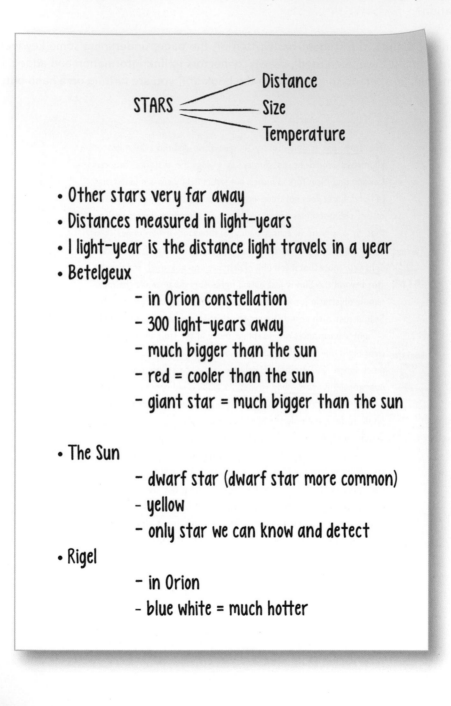

STARS — Distance
— Size
— Temperature

- Other stars very far away
- Distances measured in light-years
- 1 light-year is the distance light travels in a year
- Betelgeux
    - in Orion constellation
    - 300 light-years away
    - much bigger than the sun
    - red = cooler than the sun
    - giant star = much bigger than the sun

- The Sun
    - dwarf star (dwarf star more common)
    - yellow
    - only star we can know and detect
- Rigel
    - in Orion
    - blue white = much hotter

The third example uses a system of note-taking developed at Cornell University in America. The main notes are in the biggest box, down the side are some key words, headings, special points and then – and this is what makes the Cornell system very effective – in the box at the bottom the student summarises the main information in their own words.[23]

Distance of stars	The stars are remote. To try to give their distances in miles or kilometres would be as clumsy as giving the distance between London and New York in inches, but fortunately there is a better unit to hand. Light does not travel instantaneously; it flashes along at the rate of 186,000 miles per second (300,000 kilometres per second), so that in one year it covers nearly 6 thousand billion miles (9.6 thousand billion kilometres). This is what has become known as the light-year (note that it is a unit of distance and not time). The nearest star beyond the Sun is just over 4 light-years away, while the most remote objects so far recorded are over 12 billion light-years from us. Seen across such vast distances, the stars shine merely as tiny points of light. Appearances are deceptive; many of the stars visible on any clear night are not only much more luminous than the Sun, but also
Size	much larger. For example, Betelgeux in the constellation of Orion, over 300 light-years away, is vast. Its globe could contain the entire orbit of the Earth round the Sun. Some features have been detected on its surface, but only the Sun is near enough to be studied in real detail – and much of our knowledge of the stars in general depends upon what we have learned from studying our own neighbourhood
Dwarfs and Giants	star. Fortunately, the Sun is a very normal star, neither particularly powerful nor particularly feeble, and certainly not as variable as many. Astronomers rank it as a dwarf, but in fact it seems to be slightly more massive than the average – and giant stars such as Betelgeux are much less numerous than the dwarfs. We can also gain a great deal of understanding by looking at the colours of the stars. Just as we talk of objects being red- or white-hot, with white-hot objects being hotter than red-hot ones, so the colours of the stars reflect their temperatures. Betelgeux, for example, appears red because
Temperature – red, white, blue	it is cooler than our own Sun, whereas Rigel – the other bright star in Orion – is blue-white and is much hotter than our own, yellow Sun, which is intermediate in temperature as well as in size.

The sun is a dwarf star. Dwarf stars are more common than giant stars. Other stars are huge distances away – measured in light-years e.g. Betelgeux is 300 light-years away. Colours tell you about star temperatures: red – yellow – blue – white

Take responsibility for your own learning

The last example is a mind map. Some people believe that mind maps can be made even better if they are coloured and have small pictures added to them.

Which of the examples do you like best? You should try them all. Perhaps you could use a bit of each and develop your own style?

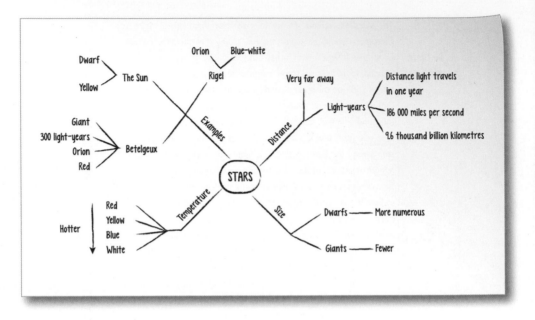

Electronic note-taking

Electronic notes have several advantages if you have access to a computer and, better still, if you have an iPad or some other tablet:

- They can easily be returned to, updated and improved.
- They can have pictures and text from the internet quickly included.
- They can be set up to facilitate revising (see below).
- They can be shared.
- They can be synched across several devices; even when you are away from your own device(s) you can retrieve your notes online.

However, whether hand-written or digital, your notes must be your own work to be meaningful. Simply cutting and pasting a chunk of text from the internet and calling it your note won't help your learning.

It is, of course, fairly easy to combine hand-written and digital notes. Your first, hand-written version can be scanned into a computer, creating a pdf file, which can then be annotated if you have the right program.

If you want some or all of your notes to be electronic in form then you can certainly use a conventional word processor, such as Word or Pages. These programs make it easy to use numbered or bulleted points and you can set up a page in the Cornell format (see above) if that is the style you want.

PowerPoint, Keynote, Prezi and other presentation software, all of which are used in schools nowadays, are also very good for note-taking. Each slide can contain the key points that you want to remember. Using the Stars example from above, you could have this:

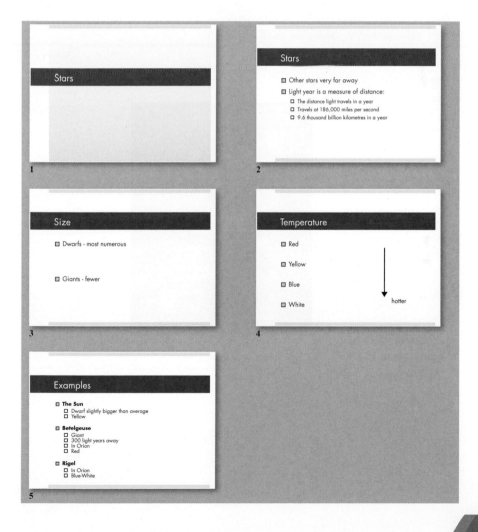

If you prepare your notes in this way, you can play them back to yourself, slide by slide and bullet point by bullet point.

But you should also look at the specialised note-taking programs that are available. They allow you to clip information from other sources into your note, to set up the page as you want it and even to draw and write on the page using your finger or a special pen.

Here are two examples which are very popular, work across all devices, PC or Mac, and in their basic form (which is probably all you need) are free.

OneNote is produced by Microsoft and integrates perfectly with Office as you would expect. Here is an example:

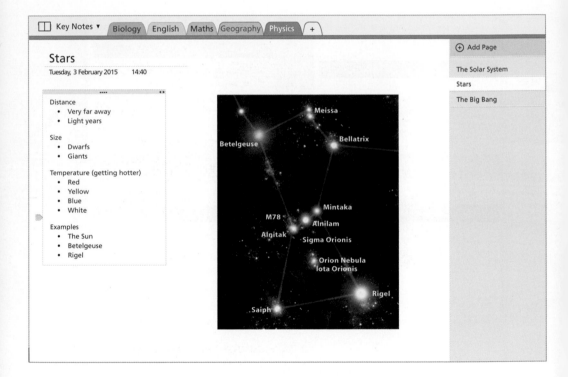

You can:

- Create notebooks. This one is called Key Notes.
- Create sections within notebooks, indicated by the tabs. This one has a section for each subject being studied
- Create as many notes as you like within each section. This one is our familiar Stars note. On the right hand side you can see this student also has notes on the solar system and the Big Bang.
- Add additional material. This student has added a picture of the Orion constellation showing Betelgeuse and Rigel.

Stars

Distance
- Very far away
- Light years

Size
- Dwarfs
- Giants

Temperature (getting hotter)
- Red
- Yellow
- Blue
- White

Take responsibility for your own learning

OneNote is a very powerful, useful piece of software, as is Evernote. Evernote also has notebooks and sections to keep your notes perfectly filed. You can also tag your notes with key words, so that they can be easily found.

There are also very good free electronic mind-mapping packages. Type 'mind-mapping software' into Google and you will find examples.

Remember that it is the actual process of thinking about what you're studying, and deciding how to summarise it in your own words, that really matters in note-taking. This is the hard bit and must not be avoided if you are going to benefit from the exercise. If you are just going to play about with attractive software you will do better using a pencil and a sheet of boring paper for your note-taking!

Practise, practise, practise

Practise, practise, practise

M-C McInally and Eric Summers

M-C McInally and Eric Summers are experienced authors and head teachers. They have written two best-selling books on Study Skills and regularly speak at conferences on this subject.

Introduction

This chapter is about practising[24]. That means we can learn a lot from sport. In sport no one questions that to be successful you have to practise. In golf, for example, players talk about 'grooving' their swing. This means that it never varies. It is so fixed and steady that, even in big competitions where golfers can come under tremendous pressure, it remains the same. They have confidence that it will always do what it is expected to do.

It is the same with actors who practise their lines so they do not forget them when on stage. Or ballet dancers who spend hour after hour going over their moves so that they do not fall down when making a spectacular jump in front of a paying audience. You get the picture?

In any activity where you want to be sure you will do well, you have to practise. Why would it be different for studying? How good it would be if, under the great pressure that exams bring, we could sit down, open the paper and know that our knowledge is not going to let us down. Practise can do that for you.

Let's think a little about what is going on here and remember the earlier chapter about knowing how your brain works.

All through your life your brain is absorbing information. As it takes in new facts and experiences it makes connections with similar information it already holds. If it is frequently reviewing these connections, they become stronger and stronger. They have been likened to your brain starting with a footpath, turning it into a road and then into a motorway. The motorway is the super connection. It is very solid, very reliable and information travels along it very fast. The professional golfer's swing is on a motorway.

Some of the knowledge you need to pass exams is unfortunately sitting along a footpath, perhaps even becoming overgrown with vegetation. You need to get it onto a motorway and then maintain that motorway. That's what practice does. It turns the connections in your brain from paths into motorways and then it keeps the motorways in a good state of repair thereafter.

Paths, roads and motorways are, of course, metaphors for what is going on in your brain. Another way of looking at it is to think of a dense ball of steel wire buzzing and flashing as information is transferred every which way through it. The more connections there are, the more wires there are, the denser the ball will be. Dense does not mean stupid here. Dense in this metaphor is good because it means you have a lot of connections. Practice will increase the density of your connections.

The trouble is that connections can weaken as well as strengthen. Motorways can revert back to being footpaths if they are not used. The connection will probably always be there but it can become very weak and, in effect, you will have forgotten what you once knew. Sadly we can all forget very quickly.

It seems that the brain has both a short-term and a long-term memory. The short-term, or working, memory, is what we need as we go about our daily business. We remember that we are opening the fridge door in order to take out a bottle of milk. We remember that today we must buy a new pair of earphones as we pass the supermarket. And then we quickly forget this type of information because we do not need it anymore. It is no longer relevant.

Unfortunately, we also forget stuff that *is* relevant and we should be trying to remember, like stuff that we are going to need to pass exams! Even if we are very attentive in class, we all quickly forget the detail of what we were told or were supposed to be learning. If the lesson bored us, if we were not concentrating, we forget even more quickly. Every teacher will tell you how he or she despairs that what was taught to pupils one day seems to have been forgotten by the next. What is going on here?

Neuroscientists believe that we cannot leave important information (and what you are taught in class is important) in our short-term memory. It has to be driven deep down into our long-term memory. Once it is in there it doesn't get forgotten. Knowing how to swim, or drive a car, or tie shoelaces, or, in the case of the professional golfer, swing a golf club – these are things that do not get forgotten because they are in your long-term, not your short-term, memory. You might forget that the battle of Hastings was fought in 1066, but the History teacher never will, because that fact is firmly in her long-term memory. For many of her pupils, however, it was always only in their short-term memory. It was never connected to a motorway. It was just like the milk taken out of the fridge. Quickly forgotten.

But it would not have been if using the information had been practised. Practice gets information – knowledge, understanding and skills – into our long-term memories. That's where we build motorways and that's what we want for exam success.

How to practise

Here are some key elements of good practising:
- It has to challenge you.
- It has to be the right sort.
- It has to be regular.

Practice should be challenging

Think about lifting weights in a gym. If you find it quite a struggle to lift a weight, it is doing you good. It is 'challenging' your body and the strain involved in making the lift builds muscle. If you can lift the weight easily, it is not doing much good because it is not putting any pressure on your body. That is why people keen to build a muscular physique steadily increase the amount they are lifting. They keep up the challenge.

So, if you want to be good at maths, there is no point spending hours adding two to two and getting it right every time (hopefully!) You know the answer is four. It is deep in your long-term memory. You need to work on problems that are difficult. Problems that force you to think. That will put pressure on your brain like heavier weights put pressure on your muscles.

It has to be the right sort[25]

This means that you should study for a decent length of time, pushing yourself (as explained above), but you must also employ the best study techniques. Here's an extreme example: there is no point practising essay writing if it is your maths you want to improve; you will have to work on maths problems to do that.

Your teacher knows which skills relating to his subject pupils find hardest to master. He knows the key knowledge that is essential to an understanding of the subject. These are what you should be practising. Until you have them 'grooved'!

> **Key Point**
>
> Don't waste time revising what you already know. Revise what you don't know. Revise what is not in your long-term memory.

The 'right sort' of studying also means paying attention to the best way to get information into our long-term memory. Why study using out-of-date methods, when we know that there are new approaches which will prove much more effective? Try to make use of the latest thinking on effective studying.

It has to be regular

On the face of it, there is nothing particularly 'modern' about studying regularly. The ancient Greeks could have told you that practising now and then, when you feel like it, is no good. There has to be a rhythm to studying, a routine, and you must stick to it. What we know now, however, is that how we structure that routine is very important.

> **Key Point**
>
> Take advice and study the right things for each subject. Be up to date in how you study.

Here is a simple exercise. Give yourself 10 minutes to memorise this poem. Concentrate very hard for the 10 minutes. Do not allow any other thought to intrude.

(Good exercise this because it's a poem well worth knowing off by heart. Nelson Mandela used it to help himself stay positive when he was in prison. Additional exercise: check who Mandela was, who wrote the poem and which film it was used in. Make connections.)

Practise, practise, practise

Invictus

Out of the night that covers me,
Black as the pit from pole to pole,
I thank whatever gods may be
For my unconquerable soul.

In the fell clutch of circumstance
I have not winced nor cried aloud.
Under the bludgeonings of chance
My head is bloody, but unbowed.

Beyond this place of wrath and tears
Looms but the Horror of the shade,
And yet the menace of the years
Finds and shall find me unafraid.

It matters not how strait the gate,
How charged with punishments the scroll,
I am the master of my fate,
I am the captain of my soul.

Do not look at the poem again for five or six hours. Then try to write out the poem. There will probably be gaps. Lines forgotten. Words missed out. Don't be tempted to go back to the original. Just leave your copied out version until tomorrow. Then go back to it. You will probably find that you can now fill in some of the gaps and do some other corrections.

What is going on here? How can it be that after 24 hours you can remember more than you did after five hours?

The problem is that the poem is not yet in your long-term memory. It is still sitting in your short-term memory. When you first copied it out you wrote down what was still sitting in your short-term memory. Then, without you realising it, the various connections in your brain were flashing away for the next 20 hours and more bits came back to you. They were still there.

But, had you waited five days before going back to the poem, you almost certainly would have found nothing left to retrieve. The memory would have faded away.

Regular practice is all about getting information into your long-term memory from which it can always be retrieved. So, what is the best way to do that?

LRP × 3

Remember this formula. It is the secret to mastering a subject. Here's what it stands for.

L = Learning

R = Revising

P = Practising

And the 3 means you have to do each three times. Let's look at this in more detail.

Stage 1: Learning

The latest research suggests that the brain needs to learn, or be taught, new information or a new skill, three times for it to really sink in. Ideally the learning should take place in three different ways with breaks in between.

Imagine a lesson where you are told something by the teacher. It is highly likely that you will quickly forget the facts you have been given, or will lose the understanding you momentarily had, if the teacher then moves on to something else.

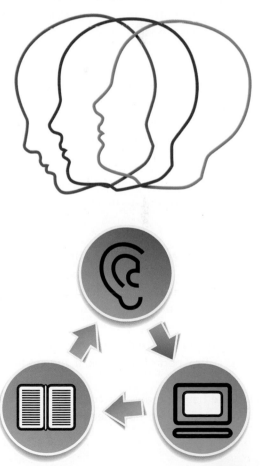

Imagine, however, that the teacher *tells* you about, say, the process of photosynthesis, goes on to something else for ten minutes, but then comes back to photosynthesis and *shows* you a five minute film clip about it. Following another short activity she return to photosynthesis for a third time and has you *read* a couple of pages in a text book and answer a few questions on the subject. Then, especially if you have been paying attention, you will leave the class understanding the basics of photosynthesis.

Practise, practise, practise

Many teachers structure their lessons in this way and that is very helpful to the student. Others tell you once and expect you to 'get it'. They are not being helpful. If we are trying to learn so that the knowledge and understanding gets properly into our long-term memory, then most of us need to learn it three times, preferably in three different ways, before the new ideas really sink in.

What if your teacher is not helpful and you leave the class not understanding the topic you have just been taught? You could of course try speaking to the teacher on your own. It is a poor teacher who does not want to talk to a pupil about their subject. But if you do not want to do that, then you must as soon as possible – that very day – go over the topic again by yourself. You could, for example, read over what Wikipedia has to say about it. In the case of photosynthesis, you would certainly find a film clip on the internet which would show you the process. And you could talk over it with another pupil in the class or, better still, an older pupil who is doing the same subject.

If you did these things, then you would be learning about photosynthesis three times in three different ways and you would be well on your way to feeling confident about the topic.

> ### Key Point
>
> So, the first key messages for learning a new topic and getting it into your long-term memory so it is never forgotten, are: **learn it three times; in three different ways; and do so quickly, preferably within 24 hours.**

Stage 2: Revising

Stage 1 was about learning a new topic. It was about properly understanding it as well as remembering the key information. Stage 2 is about reinforcement, driving the new ideas deep into your long-term memory, so that they stay with you for life (and certainly for the exams).

This is what revision does and again three is the number to remember. Each time you revise the topic the stronger your memory will become and the better your understanding will be. You are helping your brain to process the new topic, getting it catalogued, filed and connected, so that it is ready for you to use whenever you need it (in the exam, for example!).

So, when do your revise and how do you revise? We must get this right. This is perhaps the most critical part of this book. If you get this right you will transform your exam prospects.

Despite having grasped a concept and understood a bunch of facts, we can all still forget very quickly. If we have been concentrating then, a short time after we have been given information, we will probably remember it better than immediately after we were given it. This is the brain absorbing what it has learned. But then there is a very rapid falling away. One day after a lesson a great part of it will be forgotten. A week later there will be little recollection of what it was about (though if you applied the three-part learning advice more will be retained than otherwise).

But if we implement a three-part revision process, especially if it follows three-part learning, we will prevent this happening.

Here is what you must do. Look carefully at this table:

	When	Notes
Initial learning	Within 24 hours of first being introduced to a new topic	This is the 3-part learning process, getting your head round a topic by going over it in three different ways, e.g.: teacher telling you; you watching a film clip; you reading a book. Intense concentration throughout.
First revision	One day later	Take 10 minutes to go over the topic again. Read your notes or the pages in your textbook.
Second revision	One week later	Spend another 10 minutes repeating above.
Third revision	Three weeks later	Spend 5 to 10 minutes skimming your notes. If anything is unclear then you must set more time aside to read everything thoroughly once more. However, if you have completed the earlier stages properly, and if you have been *using* the information (see stage 3 below) then 5 minutes should be enough to keep everything fresh in your long-term memory.

In order to implement this approach you do have to be very well organised. You could easily bamboozle yourself and so a revision calendar is very helpful.

Refer back to the timetable in 'Stage 3: building a weekly timetable' (chapter 5, pages 69–72). Check the 'L' column on the right hand side. This can be used to check whether this is initial learning, first, second or third revision. A simple L, R1, R2, R3 code could be used to identify the study action (SA). Below is a more detailed version of such a checklist. You decide what the days are corresponding to 1–7.

Topic/Day	1		2		3		4		5		6		7
	SA	Mins	SA	Mins	SA	Mins	SA	Mins	SA	Mins	SA	Mins	
Subject 1													
Topic A											R3	5	
Topic B			R2	10									
Topic C	L	20			R1	10							
Subject 2													
Topic A													
Topic B													
Topic C							L						
Subject 3													
Topic A													
Topic B													
Topic C			L										
Subject 3													
Topic A													
Topic B													
Topic C	L												
Subject 4													
Topic A									L				
Topic B													
Topic C													
Subject 5													
Topic A													
Topic B													
Topic C											L		
Subject 6													
Topic A													
Topic B													
Topic C					L								

(Column 7: DAY OFF)

Stage 3: Practising

How do you become really good at something? By really good we mean international class. The answer from research seems to be to practise for 10,000 hours over ten years.[26] Think what that means. One thousand hours of practising every year means three hours every day. Do that and, in a decade's time, you undoubtedly will be excellent at your chosen activity.

But 10,000 hours of practice in 10 years is beyond most of us. What we have to remember is that more practise, even if it is well short of the magic 10,000 hours, will make us better. We will not get better by not practising at all!

So, with regard to studying, what are we talking about? This is what the serious research now tells us definitely makes a difference to your learning.

1. You need to know stuff, make connections and reflect on what you are learning

It sometimes seems that 'facts' is a dirty word in education. It is 'skills' and 'understanding' that are stressed. Courses must have the factual content reduced so that more time is available for learning skills.

But you need facts to develop understanding. The more facts you know the easier it is to set new information in context and to make the connections in your brain which are so important to learning. Knowing plenty of factual information about a topic gives you confidence, widens and deepens your understanding, makes it much easier to make sense of the next new topic you go on to, and it underpins the skills that of course you do wish to acquire.

When you are given new facts, pause, think about them, try to link them to other information you already know (quite deliberately help your brain to make those connections) and give yourself some time to reflect on their significance.

Think of these facts as new data that has to be processed before being stored in the computer that is your brain.

2. Space your revision

Imagine you are revising five subjects. You could spend three hours on subject A (because you really are very industrious!) on Monday evening, three hours on subject B on Tuesday and so on through to Friday.

Or you could spend 30 minutes on each subject every night (leaving 30 minutes over for breaks as you switch from one subject to the other).

Which would be the better approach?

If it is the night before the exam and you know nothing, then you'd better spend three hours cramming the subject.

Otherwise, there is no dispute, the second approach, spreading out your revision of each subject, will in the longer term yield the better results. You will remember the facts better and your understanding will be increased.

Not convinced? Does this seem a very stop-start approach, stopping after 30 minutes when you are just getting into something? Read on!

3. Interleave your revision and interrupt your learning

Although this may seem to make no sense and contradicts what was written earlier about concentration, carefully conducted experiments with students have revealed that 'interleaving' is a very effective method of revision. Of course, when you are studying you must concentrate as hard as you can, but we can only do that for a relatively short space of time. The brain actually responds to being interrupted and, in the longer term, benefits from switching from one subject to another.

Even within one subject interleaving topics has been shown to improve remembering. Let us take English literature as an example. You want to really get your head round *Hamlet*. You will actually do better to work on *Hamlet* for 20 minutes, then switch, say, to T.S. Eliot's poetry for a period of time, before coming back for another go at *Hamlet*.

Just as spacing your learning so that you are regularly coming back to a subject works, so does interrupting yourself and interleaving your topics and subjects.

Hard to believe? Try it for a couple of weeks and see.

4. Keep testing yourself

Here is another revision tip that might surprise you – we need more testing!

But we need to think about testing in a different way. It is not just about getting marks for a report card. Testing should actually be seen as part of the learning process, a method of getting vital information into your long-term memory and training your brain's retrieval systems.

Imagine you have half an hour to memorise a poem. You could try this with *Invictus* again. Which approach is better to adopt? Should you read it over and over again, perhaps using a highlighter pen, for 30 minutes? That's what most students do. The problem is, it doesn't work very well.

Much better is to read the poem with all the concentration you can muster for 10 minutes and then spend the next 20 trying to remember it – saying it out loud, writing it down, trying to fill in the blanks. The effort you make for the 20 minutes will actually fix the poem in your memory more effectively than simply staring at it for the full half hour.

Space your learning. Come back to the poem tomorrow and then next week, sticking with the second approach. The research is very clear. You will do far better than the student who simply reads the poem over and over again, especially if he doesn't come back to it. Using the second approach is harder work (see below) but the learning you will have achieved will be so much better.

Testing gives you feedback. It gives you information on what you know and what you do not. It exercises your brain far more than simply reading over notes. So don't wait for the teacher to issue tests. Test yourself … and a superb way to do that is to use flash cards. You will certainly have come across them but did you know that 40 years ago a German journalist particularly interested in the science of memory developed a very powerful flash card system? It is called Leitner Boxes[27] and it incorporated the testing and spaced learning/revision which is being so strongly recommended in this book.

The flash cards are in four boxes. Box 1 has the cards with information you don't know. Answer a card correctly and you can put it into box 2, otherwise it stays in box 1. Answer a card in box 2 correctly and you put it into box 3. Answer a card from box 3 correctly and you can put it into box 4. Box 4 therefore contains the flash cards that you know best. If you get a card wrong from box 4, you must drop it down a box. So too with boxes 3 and 2.

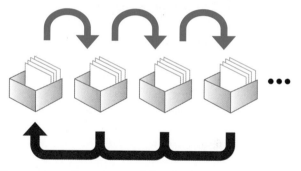

Go through your box 1 cards very frequently, box 2 a little less so, box 3 less so still, and box 4 least frequently. Leitner boxes are very effective and also great fun. The more you get the answers correct, the more your confidence is boosted. And nowadays, if you go online, you will find there are plenty of programs, some of them free, that will put flashcards on your computer, tablet or smartphone (that incorporate the Leitner method).

Testing yourself frequently has been scientifically proven to be one of the most powerful aids to learning. Your brain likes it in great part because it is harder work that just staring at a page of notes. Read on!

5. Make it hard

Real learning and meaningful revision is all about pushing yourself. There used to be an old saying that if the medicine doesn't taste unpleasant it isn't doing you any good. Be that as it may, what *is* true is that if the learning and the revision aren't hard they're not doing you much good.

Practise, practise, practise

This takes us back to an earlier point in chapter 6 on taking responsibility for your own learning. A big part of that is accepting the challenge, being willing to make it hard for yourself, so that you can make genuine progress. Spacing your learning, concentrating intensely but then interrupting yourself by interleaving and testing, testing and testing yourself again, focusing on what you do not know, is how to achieve deep learning. Giving yourself problems to solve, practising, practising, practising, that's what it is all about.

Hard? Yes it is. But it really does work.

The most important practice, however, is actually doing exam questions. You must get hold of past exam papers for each of your subjects. Study them. This is not to 'question spot', which is always dangerous, but to become totally familiar with the sort of questions that are asked. If you make sure you can answer all the questions that have been asked over the last three years, then whatever is asked this year is not going to be a great surprise.

When you do past papers you are:

1 ensuring you will not throw away silly marks in the final exam by not understanding the structure of the paper;

2 revising all the key information that you will need to have at your fingertips;

3 practising the discipline of writing to time limits;

4 making revision much harder than just staring at notes;

5 testing yourself.

Remember!

- When you are learning a new topic, go over it three times with intervals between each revision; draw up a schedule to ensure you stick to this. Remember LRP x 3.
- Make sure you then revise what you have learned. Revision should be done three times as well, with intervals and according to a schedule.
- Don't revise what you know you know; concentrate on what you are unsure of.
- Keep testing. Do past papers. Be familiar with questions and increasingly answer them against the clock.
- Keep challenging yourself; if what you are doing is easy you are not learning. If you can easily write 200 words for an answer, aim to write 300.

M-C McInally and Eric Summers

M-C McInally and Eric Summers are experienced authors and head teachers. They have written two best-selling books on Study Skills and regularly speak at conferences on this subject.

Introduction

All the organisation, all the time management, all the focus on remembering and understanding, all the practice – all will count for nothing if you do not deliver on the day. Is that what you think? Then think again!

If you have studied and learned, as this book has been encouraging you to do, then that is most definitely not time wasted. You will have changed as a person. You will have a different mindset. You will be more knowledgeable, more disciplined, a more mature and rounded individual than you were before.

If you have been following the advice on sensible eating and regular exercising, you will also be a healthier individual. In every way you will be better equipped to take on the world and make a good life for yourself. If you have been preparing as has been recommended, you will have 'capital in your bank' that you will be able to draw upon in the future. That can't be taken away from you.

But, of course, you do want to pass your exams, and pass them well, and at the first time of asking. So, having put in all the preparatory work, let's try to get it right on the day, just like the athlete in a World Championship final, or the footballer on his international debut, or the singer and the actor when they finally walk on stage.

So, here are some things to consider in the final run-up, in the last few days before the exams.

The last lap

Final honing

Over the winter, athletes concentrate on stamina work, building up the strength required for the physical demands of running fast. As the season gets closer they do more speed work, sharpening themselves up, building on the reserves they have put in the tank over the previous months.

You should have been like such athletes. Over the winter you should have been doing the hard grind of reading, writing, problem-solving and experimenting in order to widen and deepen your knowledge and understanding of the subjects you are studying, so that the key information is now deep in your long-term memory ready to be retrieved as necessary.

Now, as the exams get closer and closer, you should be doing your speed work, sharpening up what you have learned so it is ready for immediate action. Focus more and more on what is likely to be in the exam. Go over and over past exam papers. Do time trials, which means doing questions against the clock, timing yourself to complete your answers in the same time that you will have in the exam itself.

Don't practise what you know you know. Practise any last remaining parts of the course that you are still unsure of.

Speak to your teacher

Teachers are there to help. They want you to do well. So, get over any reluctance you may have and speak to your teacher about anything you still find difficult. He or she will give you time. You will not be turned away. Plug that gap in your learning that has been bothering you. You should probably have sorted it ages ago. Do it now.

Sleep

You must continue to look after yourself. It is tempting to abandon the healthy routines that have been keeping you going over the winter, but that is the last thing you should do. Exams are physically as well as mentally demanding and you need to stay fit if you are going to give of your best.

Sleep is crucial (read all about this in chapter 3). We need an average of eight hours of sleep on a regular basis. If young people have less than that, they pay a price. You can do with less sleep occasionally, but ultimately it catches up on you.

In the run-up to the exams you can lose sleep because you are trying to cram in extra study time. That is very understandable. But how well will you learn if you pressurise yourself in this way? And will any little extra knowledge you gain be outweighed by feeling rotten during the exam?

Promise yourself decent sleeps before the exams and deal with your other concerns by thinking about mindset, confidence and self-belief (you can do this!).

Confidence

Confidence is not about being arrogant and it does not mean you are unrealistic about your chances of doing well (be 'realistically positive'! – see page 7). What it means is that if you have worked hard for your exams, done what you should have done, been conscientious, tried your best, then you are entitled to enter the exam room believing you can do well.

If you have studied the past exam papers, then it is most unlikely you will be given a question that is completely different from anything that has been asked before. The style of the paper, the timings, even the colour of the paper should be quite familiar.

And confidence means you are determined to do your best.

So, the night before, you *should* sleep the sleep of the just and you owe it to yourself to be calm as you sit down to tackle the question paper. You should be alert, ready to show what you can do, but at ease with yourself. Not anxious. Not scared. Just confident you can do this.

Company

As the exams come nearer, you should give some thought to the company you keep – who is 'on your team' (see page 12). Some people will be thoroughly decent friends most of the time but, where exams are concerned, they can be a negative influence.

- There may be the friend who does want to do well but is going about it in completely the wrong way and whose bad habits can rub off on you.
- There may be the friend who just seems good at everything, knows they are going to sail through the exams and, without trying to do so, makes you feel inferior.
- There may be the friend who is studying hard but is very negative and pessimistic, with a low mood which communicates itself to you.
- There may be the friend who himself has no interest in exam success, has no intention of working for exams and doesn't want you to either.

Whatever excuse you have to make use it and, until the exams are over, avoid these friends. You can catch up with them later and you will enjoy doing so all the more if you know you did not allow them to distract you from your exam preparation.

Equipment

Do you have everything you need? Don't leave it till the last minute. If your old calculator is not reliable, get a new one now. Having everything ready well in advance will help head off last minute panics which can undermine your confidence.

Checklists

The checklist is an amazingly simple yet astonishingly powerful idea. Using a checklist is not a sign that you cannot remember things for yourself. It doesn't indicate that you are in need of guidance because you do not understand what you are doing. A checklist is just a tool which helps us ensure that important things get done, that important stages in a process are not forgotten, that we are as prepared as we possibly can be.

Life can be very complicated at times. Often we seem to be juggling many balls in the air. Checking that something has not been missed out is just sensible.

Imagine you are sitting in a plane, waiting to take off. You want to be confident that the pilot knows what he or she is doing. You want be sure that the plane is safe to fly in and that the pilot has checked that everything is in working order. Now, the pilot will be highly intelligent and very well trained. But he or she is still just a human being and so could easily make a mistake. A vital check might be overlooked. Pilots make sure this does not happen by using a simple checklist. They go through everything that needs to be checked, ticking off the list as they go, and only then do they take you into the air.

Atul Gawande, a writer and surgeon, has written about the humble checklist. Surgery is another very complicated business and can last for hours. If you were going under the knife, would you not want to be confident that the surgeon, another highly intelligent, highly trained professional, hasn't forgotten anything? It would be very easy to do so. Gawande explains that among all the expensive, sophisticated medical equipment, the simple checklist, read over before the first incision is made, is as important as anything else in saving people's lives.[28]

Sitting exams is complicated. There is much to remember. In the heat of the moment, no matter how well you have studied, it is so easy

My History Checklist

World War One

- [ ] Armed camp
- [ ] Schlieffen plan
- [ ] Battle of the Marne
- [ ] Trench warfare
- [ ] The Somme
- [ ] New technology
- [ ] The war at sea
- [ ] The home front
- [ ] The end of stalemate
- [ ] Armistice
- [ ] The Treaty of Versailles
- [ ] Key vocabulary
  - [ ] Salient
  - [ ] Mortar
  - [ ] Creeping barrage

to miss something really important. So get yourself some checklists. You could draw them up using the information from this book and from the course outlines that your teachers will have given you.

You could have a checklist for each subject, listing each topic in the course, the key concepts and the most important vocabulary. Include a tick box that you can check when you are sure you have revised that section.

Another category of checklist could be for the food and exercise you take. Check that you have been keeping yourself healthy.

The equipment described above, the tools for the job, should also be on a checklist. Run through it before you leave for the exam. This will ensure that you have everything with you that you need.

Most important of all, your spaced learning and revision, described in the previous chapter, can be monitored using a checklist.

A practical countdown to the exams

You have read about planning, taking responsibility for your learning, creating a study timetable, revising, practising and constructing checklists for yourself. Let's look now at putting these together into a program me that will guide you right up to the point at which you enter the exam room. We'll do it from six weeks out and we'll assume you are studying six subjects. You will have to tailor the example which follows to your own particular situation.

The aim must be to go over all the topics in all your subjects three times and also to do plenty of testing, mostly using exam type questions, preferably questions taken from past exam papers. Don't worry if that means you're re-doing questions you've tackled before. But you should be producing better answers second time round.

Weeks 6 and 5:

- Use these two weeks to go over all the topics in all your subjects. Take your time. Stay focused. Make a big effort to remember key information but especially ensure you understand everything. Interleave the topics. Keep testing yourself. Speak to your teacher about anything that still confuses you.
- Set some time aside to check over your study area again. Do you have all the equipment, books and notes you need? Sort it if you haven't.
- Decide you are going to keep exercising regularly and eating properly. Don't give up sport or other hobbies. Remember that the best studying is when you are 100% focused, but that you can only stay that way for a limited time. Breaks, fresh air and exercise are important.

Weeks 4 and 3:

- During these two weeks go over all the topics a second time. Spend approximately half the time on each topic that you did in weeks 6 and 5. Use the other half of your time to do questions from past exam papers. You could refer occasionally to your notes if you have to. Again, see your teacher if any question is sticking you.
- Check your files again. Is everything where it should be in your folders? Do you have all the past exam papers to hand?
- Review the exam timetable this week. Make absolutely sure you know the dates and timings of your various exams.
- Keep the exercise and healthy eating going. It is very easy, as you inevitably become a little more anxious, to indulge in comfort eating. Try to resist the crisps, burgers, etc.

Weeks 2 and 1:

- Go over all your topics for a third time. You should aim to again halve the time that you spend on each (i.e. a quarter of the time you spent in weeks 6 and 5). Skim over what you are sure you know. Linger on the sections that remain a little more difficult for you. Keep up the interleaving and the testing. Spend most of your time on past questions. Do a selection of answers against the clock. You don't have to do a whole paper. You can work out how many minutes should be spent on each question. For example, it might work out that you should spend eight minutes on a 4-mark question. Do that for practice. Set a stopwatch for eight minutes and do the question in that time. No notes though in this last fortnight.
- This is when you could let it go. As the exams approach you become anxious. Stay calm, keep exercising and eating properly. Don't give in to junk food.
- Stick to the plan and that will keep you working well and will reduce anxiety.
- A further tidy, check and filing hour, just so everything is in its place. See any teacher you need to go over a tricky topic with you.
- Get all the equipment required for each exam laid out and ready at the end of week 1. Keep things going, right through until every exam is finished. Don't slacken off as you near the end and don't let one bad exam put you off (or even one bad question during an exam). Pick yourself up and go on to the next exam or next question.

Summary

We are now nearing the end of this book. If you have read it through from the beginning, well done! That suggests you are serious about studying. You have been given a lot of information, much advice and a lot of suggestions as to what you should do. It's a lot to take in, so let's try to pull it all together and provide you with a summary of the key points.

Getting motivated

- Learn that to admit where you are right now is the biggest and best first step.
- Understand the power of your brain and beliefs.
- Find a way to stay positive during the challenging times at school.
- Gather a team around you that will help you make it through.
- Use time to your advantage.
- Simply #keepongoing is a key skill for your exams and life!

Know your own mind

- Each time we practise any task, we make the pathways between the neurons in our brain stronger and so the task becomes easier.
- Many factors affect how well our brain works on any particular day and one of those is stress.
- Stress is an important biological system which actually helps us perform at our best – but if stress builds up and we don't manage it properly, we can face many side-effects, such as feeling ill, performing less well, having mood swings and lacking concentration.
- So, your brain will work better (and you will be healthier and happier) if you build good de-stressing activities into *every* day.
- Everyone will find these strategies helpful, including people with extra challenges, such as dyslexia, OCD or many other situations that can make life stressful.

Look after yourself

- There are lots of simple ways to look after your brain and body so that you can perform at your best during exams and feel better.
- Exercise is a great route to a healthy brain and body – it is known to be good for stress, mood, self-esteem and learning.
- Sleep is another wonderful medicine and very necessary for both health and learning. Your sleeping brain is doing a lot of work for you!
- However, many teenagers find it hard to get enough sleep. Luckily, there's plenty of good advice to help you.
- Your brain needs the right choice of foods and plenty of liquid, ideally in the form of water. Brains don't work well when they lack fuel.
- However, when you're nervous, you may not feel like eating, so it's important to work out some foods you'll be happy to snack on in exam time.

Tackling pressure head on

- Nerves affect a lot of students preparing for their exams, but it is possible to prevent them from having a negative impact on your exam performance.
- Once you understand how and why you experience nerves it becomes easier to do something about it.
- Confidence is the biggest contributor to success. If you become more confident about your ability then it will be easier to deal with your nerves.
- Short-term strategies like listening to music and breathing exercises help tone down the effects of adrenaline.

Plan for success

- Difficult and complicated projects require careful planning. Studying is difficult and complicated and therefore requires careful planning as well.
- Time spent planning your study strategy at the beginning is not time lost. You will be repaid many times over because if you plan well you will go on to study more efficiently and effectively.
- Good planning is about knowing exactly what your commitments are, what free time you have, *when* you are going to study and *where* you are going to study.
- Good planning requires a calendar which gives you an overview, the big picture if you like, of the school year and the months leading up to the exams.
- Good planning also needs a weekly timetable which clarifies exactly what you are going to do over the coming seven days. It has to be revised every week.
- Thinking ahead is important. This means you set aside sufficient time to complete work you have been assigned and to meet all your deadlines.

Take responsibility for your own learning

- Decide you want to do well. All the books you might read on how to be successful will count for nothing. You have to decide you want to do well.
- You have to work hard to be successful. It won't be easy. You are going to need grit and determination.
- A growth mindset will help a lot. This means you have an attitude that says, 'I'm up for this challenge. I will learn from failures. I will always bounce back. I will do better next time.'
- Take responsibility for your own learning. It's *your* brain, *you* are the one sitting exams, it's about *your* future. Don't blame others if you do not do well. You should be in charge of your own learning.
- Get organised. Have all the tools for the job ready and near at hand – books, notes, pens, pencils, computing equipment, etc.

- Notes need to be kept filed so that they can be easily accessed. Loose notes get lost. Ring binders are useless without dividers.
- Part of organisation may also involve negotiating with other members of your family when you can have a room to yourself to get on with your studying.

Practise, practise, practise

- Effective studying demands concentration. Even if you do all the above, it might count for nothing if, when you sit down to work, your mind is not on the job.
- Multi-tasking is a myth. You can only really do one thing at a time. If you are serious about studying then switch off the phone, the TV, the radio and the email before you start your study session.
- It is therefore better to study in short bursts, say for half an hour and certainly for no more than an hour, and then to take a 'breather'. Get up from the desk, drink some water, walk about for a few minutes before getting back to it.
- Remember the three stage rule about learning. You need to go over topics three times, preferably in different ways, in order to get the knowledge and the understanding deep into your long-term memory.
- Space out your revision.
- Interleave topics as you study.
- Don't just stare at a page. Be active and involved in the learning process. So:
  - Read with a pencil in your hand and point to key words in the text.
  - Take notes.
  - Try problems and questions (not just what you have been set for homework).
  - Keep *thinking*. Relate what you are learning now to what you already know. Help your brain to make those connections which are so important.
  - Keep testing yourself. Testing is far better for you than just reading notes over and over again.
- Go over past exam papers.
- Ask for help. Speak to your teacher if, after giving it your best shot, you still do not understand something.

Getting ready for the exams

- As the big day approaches, stay positive and stick to your routine.
- Do not allow others to distract you or put you off.
- Check and double-check the exam timetable.
- Have everything ready the night before.
- Arrive in good time for the exam but not too early; you do not want to be standing around worrying.
- Be confident and do your best. If you have studied hard, no one can ask for more.

End notes

Chapter 1

[1] Based loosely on the words of B.J. Gallagher and Steve Ventura in their book *Who are "They" anyway?*: Kaplan Business, 2004.

Chapter 2

[2] For example, work by Daniel Weissman, Earl Miller, David Meyer and Marcel Just.

[3] A 2004 *Creativity Research Journal* (Vol. 16, No. 2.3) study found that sadness hinders new ideas. Karen Gasper, PhD, Penn State University.

[4] There is one on my website – www.nicolamorgan.com -> Teenage brain/stress – > Free breathing/relaxation audio.

[5] PISA OECD report *Do students today read for pleasure?* www.oecd.org/pisa/pisaproducts/pisainfocus/48624701.pdf.

[6] Authentic Happiness website: www.authentichappiness.sas.upenn.edu

[7] www.childline.org.uk

[8] 'Mental exercising through simple socializing: social interaction promotes general cognitive functioning'. Ybarra, O., Burnstein, E., Winkielman, P., Keller M.C., Manis, M., Chan, E., Rodriguez, J., *Personality and Social Psychology Bulletin*, 2008 Feb; 34(2): 248–59

[9] *Kindness and the Case for Altruism* by Ben Dean, www.authentichappiness.sas.upenn.edu/newsletters/authentichappinesscoaching/kindness

Chapter 3

[10] NHS website, www.nhs.uk/Livewell/fitness/Pages/Whybeactive.aspx

[11] For example, Mayo Clinic, www.mayoclinic.org/healthy-living/stress-management/in-depth/exercise-and-stress/art-20044469 and Timothy Schoenfeld et al., 'Physical exercise prevents stress-induced activation of granule neurons and enhances local inhibitory mechanisms in the dentate gyrus', *Journal of Neuroscience*, 1 May 2013.

[12] NHS advice: www.nhs.uk/Livewell/fitness/Pages/physical-activity-guidelines-for-young-people.aspx

[13] For example: 'Memory for semantically related and unrelated declarative information: the benefit of sleep, the cost of wake,' by Jessica Payne, University of Notre Dame, news.nd.edu/news/29625-learning-best-when-you-rest-sleeping-after-processing-new-info-most-effective-new-study-shows/

[14] See new work by Karunesh Ganguly of UC San Francisco, Jose M. Carmena of University of California, Berkeley and others.

[15] 'Sleep drives metabolite clearance from the adult brain', Lulu Xie et al., *Science*, 18 October 2013: Vol. 342, no. 6156, pp. 373–377

[16] Matthew Walker, UC Berkeley, senior author of study published in *Nature Communications*, 6 August 2013, newscenter.berkeley.edu/2013/08/06/poor-sleep-junk-food/

[17] 'Alcohol's effects on the adolescent brain – what can be learned from animal models', Susanne Hiller-Sturmhöfel, PhD and H. Scott Swartzwelder, PhD, http://pubs.niaaa.nih.gov/publications/arh284/213-221.htm – from the National Institute of Alcohol Abuse and Alcoholism

Chapter 5

[18] M. Currey, *Daily Rituals*, Picador, 2014

[19] B. Franklin, *The Autobiography of Benjamin Franklin*, 1791

Chapter 6

[20] C. Dweck, *Mindset*, Robinson, 2012

[21] G. Nuthall, *The Hidden Lives of Learners*, NZCER, 2007

[22] C. Lintott et al., *Bang! The Complete History of the Universe*, Carlton, 2012

[23] A pdf explaining the Cornell method for students is available at http://www.usu.edu/arc/idea_sheets/pdf/note_taking_cornell.pdf

Chapter 7

[24] For the research mentioned in this chapter, see, for example, Brown, Roediger and McDaniel, *Make it Stick: the Science of Successful Learning*, Belknap Harvard, 2014; B. Carey, *How We Learn*, Macmillan, 2014; T.M. Sterner, *The Practicing Mind*, New World Library, 2012.

[25] M. Syed, *Bounce: The Myth of Talent and the Power of Practice*, Fourth Estate, 2011. Prizewinning journalist Matthew Syed was once a champion table tennis player and wrote this wonderful book that gives insights into right (and wrong!) sorts of training and practice.

[26] M. Gladwell, *Outliers: The Story of Success*, Penguin, 2009

[27] See, for example, http://leitnerportal.com/LearnMore.aspx

Chapter 8

[28] A. Gawande, *The Checklist Manifesto*, Profile Books, 2011